VERSES ON THE VANGUARD

RUSSIAN POETRY TODAY

Verses on the Vanguard

POETRY & DIALOGUE
FROM CONTEMPORARY RUSSIA

Edited and with an Introduction by Polina Barskova

DEEP VELLUM PUBLISHING
DALLAS, TEXAS

Cover design by Sarah Schulte
Typography by Kit Schluter

ISBN: 978-1-64605-162-5
Ebook: 978-1-64605-163-2

Library of Congress Control Number: 2021950420

Contents

Introduction

POLINA BARSKOVA

Russian poetry, that whimsical appendix and/or mirror of the
Russian culture that accumulates and reflects its most urgent
reverberations, is *at it again*. As has happened in the past, for
example during the Russian fin de siècle epoch that we call the
Silver Age, various (drastically different) approaches and answers
to the question "what is a poetical text today?" cohabitate, coexist
in literary process/practice. (One might dwell here on a vision of
lions and antelopes peacefully, or almost peacefully, drinking from
the river after a drought).

Every morning my Facebook scroll brings me poems written
as if in the Soviet Union in 1972; poems written as if in a post-
Putin (God willing) Russia in 2044, in some future version of the
post-Soviet realm; and poems written as if from points all along
the historical spectrum in between. The primary purpose of this
anthology (and, hopefully, its younger siblings, the next iterations
in the series) is to capture the paradoxical and exciting coexistence
of the multiple versions of the new avant-garde and present it to
the American reader. We witness today poetry that is aggressively
political and aggressively apolitical (which is its own version of
politics); works with the form and tasks of the Russian/Soviet
Romantic lyrical intention (rhymed, metered, establishing the "I"
at its center) and works without rhyme or meter, created as if by
the observant computer camera.

How should the reader of the anthology understand the
notion of the *vanguard* that we chose to put into the title of
the anthology? The most striking impression is that the most
novel, original developments in contemporary Russian poetry

might strike us as particularly dissimilar. Maria Galina writes in traditional form, with rhyme and meter, but her texts are inhabited by aliens and zombies; Ekaterina Simonova's texts are inhabited with the literary giants like Mikhail Bulgakov and Daniil Kharms—together with the poet's ghostly grandparents and difficult girlfriends—while in the poems of Oksana Vasyakina the world is filled first and foremost with the screams and shrieks of various passions. The central observation of the witness of these vanguards is how different they are in their texture, context, purpose, and relationship to literary tradition. And it is precisely this variety, this overwhelming sense of difference that makes this moment so singularly important, novel, and exciting: one can choose how to be of the Vanguard—or of the Vanguards, since the situation appears to be so plural.

I would like to begin by introducing the poets in this volume with a case that leaves me in awe of the sheer daring and wit of its hybridizing effort and play of intellect—that of Maria Galina (translated by Ainsley Morse):

> I was at the ends of the earth
> I saw places where
> When locals gape their eyes there's nothing there,
> A man spoke with me
> Who'd taken an axe and gone after his wife
> Not because of marital strife
> But because it wasn't her. The simple ones
> Are simpler to swap out for those from other suns.
> Betelgeuse, Sirius, Achernar
> Dispense her daily ration from afar.
> By nights above the empty villages stands light,
> Sirius, can you hear, do you read me,
> He's snoring, face to the wall,
> She reports:
> Call back the landing crafts
> This earth kills even its own . . .
> Bark is splitting on the trees,
> Brass-buckle moon standing in the window's crosspiece,
> On the rise beside the empty hut
> Dead men jut like posts half driven in.

As regards the Earth-Moon dyad,
I'm the only agent left alive . . .
She hasn't mastered the subtle art of sleep.
She gets in, cautious, on her side,
Tugs at the face that tends to slip and slide,
Hears him mumbling: "bitch, I'll kill you . . ."
The tidings carry heavenward in a slantwise blaze,
Heading for the Gemini constellation.
Outside, tossing-turning, heavy—somebody.
She grabs his shoulder, shakes:
"I'm scared. Talk to me."

Galina combines very traditional form with almost shocking, "unfitting" narrative—that of sci-fi, impulse—and thus an unsettling conflict emerges between the vessel and its content, between one's expectation of comfort and the realization of eerie disturbance. Galina is a renowned sci-fi writer in Russia and elsewhere with her own signature. In her own concoction of magic realism, the realism is really real, and every time I reread her texts an uncanny comparison to Nikolai Gogol comes to mind. She depicts God-forgotten, all but deserted villages and provincial towns where everything and everybody is strange enough even without aliens, and their visit just adds melancholy and absurdity to the realm of abandonment and isolation. This is the landscape of after, where life and death become genuinely and disturbingly inseparable.

This poetry that at first strikes a reader as simple, transparent, understandable, recognizable. turns to be the space of sci-fi horror and anxiety, of fear and delusion, where nothing is what it seems, nobody is who you hope them to be—and most urgently it makes the reader question the lyrical voice itself: who is speaking? A traveler, a monster, a changeling, or maybe it is Death itself? Postapocalyptic imagination is "packaged" into traditional rhyme and meter that also create the impression of a trap.

Unlike the mysterious and deceptive versions of reality in Galina's texts, Oksana Vasyakina's poems speaks her object of choice—pain—very directly. While we can say that Galina locates the events of her writing in the abstract time and place of the timeless catastrophe, Vasyakina insists that her time of catastrophe is <u>now</u>.

The presentness and directness in Vasyakina's work are shocking. She obviously chooses to shock, to rough her reader: her poetry invents a whole world of passion (in every possible meaning of this rich word) largely absent in Russian poetry until recently—that of the LGBT protest against the state-sponsored homophobia enthusiastically supported by "collective opinion," enamored with the Putin regime's animosity toward various kinds of Otherness. Vasyakina's poetry (translated by Anna Halberstadt) is flagrantly direct, erotically charged, and even sensually aggressive, emotionally raw:

> you insert your fingers into my wet mouth
> I feel their salty taste
> And I feel the relief with my tongue, it is hard like dense cardboard
> You smell like paper
> You smell like a book
> You are a book, and my gaze glides over you
> And meanings swirl between us, we develop them
> They are red warm fiery
> We develop a meaning

Vasyakina's task is to create a new language (one might argue that this is the task of every poet, but here the task seems especially urgent)—to create a language for the erotic desire, intimacy, that kind of love that was censored out, silenced by centuries of Russian/Soviet state hypocrisy. Even when whispering, this poetry screams.

Which is not, as it turns out, the only possible tone with which to speak the queer language and cause in Russia today—as we see in the poetry of another of the anthology's contributors, Ekaterina Simonova. Curiously, both Vasyakina and Simonova are literary scholars; they study and teach literature in various capacities. Yet while Vasyakina chooses the poetics of direct utterance, of open sound, Simonova plays the role of "learned poet," always relying on literary irony, locating her experience in the specific literary tradition of the past with which she is in constant dialogue—that is of the Russian Silver Age with its homosexual demigods, Mikhail Kuzmin and Sophia Parnok.

Simonova's poetry (translated by Kevin Platt) has its unique prosaic quality: written in free verse, unrhymed, it depicts the daily life of a reader and a lover, but most crucially of an attentive observer:

> It's completely pointless to write about a quiet little pleasure.
> Nothing's more of a bore than poems about everything being fine.
> The only comfort is this: when I lie dying
> It's certain that I'll remember neither my own nor others' poetry,
>
> But this July instead, hot as a boiled teapot,
> The trout's pink meat, a fishbone nearly swallowed,
> A glass of cold chardonnay sweating with condensation,
> Timofey the cat, sorrowfully taking in the smells,
> Lena, proud of her fish and herself, repeating over and over:
> "Well I'm something aren't I? Say it: I'm something!"

The authors of the younger generation presented in the anthology (one of our purposes was to construe a dialogue of various poetic generations) write very varied versions of poetry and yet share obsessions in common, such as intense critique of the previous models of subjectivity. For example, Aleksandra Tsibulia, according to one of her readers, "explores the world as if devoid of humans," though nevertheless full of curiosity and even poignant beauty—but for whose eyes is it? In one of her poems (translated by Catherine Ciepiela), she writes:

> I deliberately take the same route I took after the explosion, across two bridges. There's the same number of people, but this time they look relaxed, obviously just "taking a stroll"; no one's forcing them, after dismounting, to cover unexpected distances. The place is filled with so-called lovers. They're crowded onto the fountains, which, with the absence of water, resemble some kind of commemorative monuments. One of my finds—a melted snowflake made of foil. Someone says "got shafted," then "totally fab." Through the mosque's minarets a full moon rises, takes the shape of clarity. Looks like it's all settled now. And I'm

also celebrating: the meager, nondescript return (after a long retreat) of speech.

Ivan Sokolov (translated by Elina Alter) goes even further in making the voice agency in his poetry as if non-, post-, a-human:

incisors , hold it , the median , chintzy and hinges , pics from shower , not thicker than ours planks pallets are hammered out of sagging in view of the passenger—trashmounds ? remainders ? unaccommodated in the dusk of apricots (a as in aspirants as in ravening accident) ? glad you wrote , warmth the enemy of beauty , dust , at night under the endarkened moon like dogs' tails blazening dreadlocks of dust , when in rheums—do like the residents , that which was written , taking place , over the lines of a nitrous script-conveyer , for new year's i wanted to give you my favorite plant when will it end regularis , wax and wildflower squashed postulates about how , to put the gopnik up against the wall for his freedom , didn't we celebrate the tally of gathering rallies of bestial happiness , i suspect someone took the bottom out from under this target , down-body and body-virtual crewing competition—just pick one , that which is written collects in that interval wait-isn't-that-the-feed-surging-in-tingles , i'll show you a vision hustling aloneliness [...]

That very explosion that precedes and thus conditions Tsibulia's act of melancholic flânerie seems to have destroyed the structure and texture of language in Sokolov's poetry world. His poetry is also about a visual scandal: it rejects what Russian poetry traditionally offered as the look of a poem. This text is visually formless, and thus it questions one of poetry's most precious obsessions: a separate, unique form.

Nikita Sungatov's poetry reads as a commentary, an ironic guide to the voluminous diversity sketched above. He plays with, probes various intonations and positions as if traveling through them, teasing them, using them as his mirrors. Sungatov's poetic voice (translated by Valeriya Yermishova) is that of a poetic jester who can produce his own speech mostly by "mocking" and reflecting that of others—yet he functions also as a collector, a bumblebee who cross-pollinates various separate obsessions, ambitions, and trajectories of poetic work/practice:

What can be said about this text? What needs to be said? A violent criminal is placed in the setting of a popular poem by Linor Goralik, which, in turn, was written on the margins of an evangelical plot. Another obvious precursor is Anna Gorenko's *My Body Followed Me My Body* ... The poem is bound together by a number of concepts: the State and the masculine subject; Christianity and Judaism; contemporary poetry and literary reality; the Arab-Israeli conflict and the Great Terror; violence and the media; violence and ideology; violence and the sacred; violence and the romanticization of it; and so on and so forth. What is the connection between these concepts? Who is the narrator in this poem? And who is speaking right now? To avoid having to answer an uncomfortable question, you must ask your interlocutor to repeat it a few times, then, declare it a banality and a cliché.

Reading these poems, these poets together, it's sometimes difficult to believe that they live, write in the same epoch—and nevertheless, taken together these voices demonstrate that strange, spacious volume of opportunities that Russophone poetry offers its practitioner today. The possibilities are many, and, crucially, they often read as critique, as commentary and reflections on one another, as happens, for example, with Vasyakina and Simonova. Their work demonstrates two radically different directions that the queer poets and queer poetry—one of the most exciting "areas" of new Russian writing—are exploring today.

Moving on, the second, equally imperative part of the anthology consists of the poets' discussions of process with their translators. If we think of translators as mirroring and amplifying devices for poets and their texts (among their many other functions), it is up to the translator to discern as if in a microscope the unique and subtle qualities of any particular poetry mechanism.

For example, addressing the workings of Tsibulia's practice in an interview with her, Catherine Ciepiela says, "I find that a real challenge for the translator is allowing the poem to keep its secrets ... With your poems, especially, I feel it's important to honor their reticence." Every translator in the anthology chooses their version of creative distance—how closely they approach the poem—and again the diversity of choices is illuminating.

The conversations between our poets and their translators in the anthology touch on many questions of importance—such as who is the poetry reader today, both in Russia and in the US? Ainsley Morse suggests an answer in her conversation with Maria Galina:

MG: To English-language readers, how familiar and comprehensible is Russian—not poetry per se, but the network of images and ideas that contemporary Russian authors refer to?

Who are the readers of Russian poetry in English translation? University students or professors of the humanities? Does anyone outside of the academy read this stuff?

AM: In my opinion there's a big difference between Russian and American readers of poetry—partly a blunt difference in numbers (I think there are objectively fewer poetry readers in the US), but it has to do with different reading cultures. If you're talking about readers of more experimental contemporary poetry, maybe the numbers are similar; but in Russia there is still just a much larger contingent of people who read poetry *voobshche* [in general] . . .

But then it's interesting to see newer Russian poetry that's more "transparent," with more overt allusions that are also less tied to a specifically Russian/Soviet historical-literary context; these differences make it simultaneously more and less satisfying to translate, you can be more confident about getting things across while also feeling like you're getting off easy . . . Still, there are definitely nonacademic readers of Russian poetry in translation. The Russian American literary communities have the best of both worlds (some frame of Russian cultural reference plus fluency in American culture). And there are English-language poets (and other readers) who find things in translated poetry that we translators don't even notice. These are my favorite readers, really, the ones who inspire me to keep translating.

Another urgent (yet eternal, accursed) question is how close or how remote a translator *should* be to or from the author in terms of experience, identity, taste, ideology and aesthetics. Kevin Platt muses on that:

In a recent reading I was asked if there were special challenges for me as a man in translating poetry written by a woman. I answered then that translation is always about stretching the bounds of your own your subjectivity. I'd like to add here that gender is the least of the challenges we face these days as translators. What about space?

This year it has been: flip open the laptop, put on your headphones, fire up Zoom, and translate.

For the first time, I've translated a living poet whom I've never met in person . . . With Ekaterina, my subjectivity was stretched in completely new ways—geographically, politically, linguistically, and every which way.

I think one of our anthology's credos is that of acknowledging, savoring difference, taking one's creative subjectivity to its furthest im/possible horizon where poets and translators meet each other and their new, future selves and versions and words.

POLINA BARSKOVA is a poet, scholar, and author of twelve collections of poems and two books of prose in Russian. She has also authored a monograph, *Besieged Leningrad: Aesthetic Responses to Urban Disaster* (2017), and edited three scholarly volumes. Her collection of creative nonfiction, *Living Pictures*, received the Andrei Bely Prize in 2015, was published in German with Suhrkamp Verlag, and is forthcoming in English with New York Review Books. She edited the Leningrad Siege poetry anthology *Written in the Dark* (Ugly Duckling Presse) and has four collections of poetry published in English translation: *This Lamentable City* (Tupelo Press), *The Zoo in Winter* (Melville House), *Relocations* (Zephyr Press), and *Air Raid* (Ugly Duckling Presse). She has taught at Hampshire College, Amherst College, and Smith College and now teaches Russian literature at the University of California, Berkeley.

Poems by Maria Galina

TRANSLATED BY AINSLEY MORSE

MARIA GALINA is a poet, translator, and critic. She has published several collections of poetry as well as novels and short stories. Educated as a biologist (specializing in marine biology), Galina changed careers in the 1990s, becoming a professional translator and writer. Since 2010 she has worked for the literary journal *Novyi mir*. As a poet she became well known in the late 1990s; in 2006 her poetry collection *Nonearth* won the Novyi mir Anthology prize (for a major contribution to the development of Russian poetry), as well as the Moscow Reckoning prize for best poetry book published in Moscow of the year. (She received this prize a second time in 2015 for the verse novel *Everything about Liza*). Galina has taken part in international poetry festivals, and her poetry has been translated into several languages. As a translator she works on contemporary English-language (Fiona Sampson, Ruth Padel, Charles Simic, Carol Ann Duffy) and Ukrainian (Marianna Kiyanovskaya, Vasyl' Makhno, Serhiy Zhadan, Galina Kruk) poetry. As a literary scholar she works on the social aspects of genre; she has also authored several collections of literary criticism, mostly on speculative fiction.

AINSLEY MORSE is a translator of both Russian and former Yugoslav literature and a professor at Dartmouth College. Morse's previous publications include translations of Vsevolod Nekrasov, Andrei Egunov-Nikolev, and Yury Tynianov. Most recently, she coedited *F-Letter*, an anthology of contemporary Russian feminist poetry (isolarii, 2020).

Я была на краю земли
Я видела такие места,
Где из глаз местных жителей выглядывает пустота,
Говорил со мной
Человек, который гонялся с топором за своей женой
Не потому, что она была ему неверна,
А потому, что это была не она. Того, кто прост
Проще подменить существам со звезд.
Бетельгейзе, Сириус, Процион
Ей отмеряют суточный рацион.
По ночам над пустыми селами стоит свет,
Сириус, как слышишь, прием, прием,
Он храпит, отвернувшись лицом к стене,
Она передает:
Отзовите десантные катера
Эта земля убивает даже своих . . .
На деревьях лопается кора,
Бляшка луны в крестовине окна стоит,
На пригорке подле пустой избы
Мертвецы стоят, как вкопанные столбы.
Применительно к паре Земля-Луна
Из всех разведчиков выжила я одна . . .
Она не владеет тонким искусством сна.
Она осторожно пристраивается на краю,
Поправляет расползшееся лицо,
Слышит, как он бормочет – сука, убью . . .
Весть уносится в небо косым лучом,
В направленье созвездия Близнецов.
Кто-то тяжелый ворочается за стеной.
Она трясет его за плечо:
- Мне страшно. Поговори со мной.

I was at the ends of the earth
I saw places where
When locals gape their eyes there's nothing there,
A man spoke with me
Who'd taken an axe and gone after his wife
Not because of marital strife
But because it wasn't her. The simple ones
Are simpler to swap out for those from other suns.
Betelgeuse, Sirius, Achernar
Dispense her daily ration from afar.
By nights above the empty villages stands light,
Sirius, can you hear, do you read me,
He's snoring, face to the wall,
She reports:
Call back the landing crafts
This earth kills even its own . . .
Bark is splitting on the trees,
Brass-buckle moon standing in the window's crosspiece,
On the rise beside the empty hut
Dead men jut like posts half driven in.
As regards the Earth-Moon dyad,
I'm the only agent left alive . . .
She hasn't mastered the subtle art of sleep.
She gets in, cautious, on her side,
Tugs at the face that tends to slip and slide,
Hears him mumbling: "bitch, I'll kill you . . ."
The tidings carry heavenward in a slantwise blaze,
Heading for the Gemini constellation.
Outside, tossing-turning, heavy—somebody.
She grabs his shoulder, shakes:
"I'm scared. Talk to me."

из поэмы «Все о Лизе»

Спасатель Коля Рассказывает Что Он Видел

я водил поход по родному краю
с пионерским приветом и все такое
после двух привалов своей рукою
перерезал бы спиногрызов
(у меня есть золинген видишь Лиза)
верещат и носятся вот зараза
а у нас экология и заказник
листоед *Cecchiniola* редкий эндемик[1]
в каждом ручье ручейник а это Лиза
индикатор отсутствия загрязненья
здесь у нас под каждым кустом дриада
под каждым листом цикада
и нефиг тут орать в натуре

я вообще-то к детям не так уж плохо
но у нас тэбэ а они лезут
причем все разом.

> *говорят дети:*
> когда выходишь
> из воды сразу
> такая тяжесть
> такая радость
> столько света
> соль на коже
> если это
> не рай так что же

---

1. Кстати Лиза самый крупный кузнечик нашего края из отряда прямокрылых (Orthopetra) - дыбка степная (Saga pedo Pall) размножается партеногенетически и самцы на данной территории не встречаются. Размеры самок этого вида от головы до конца яйцеклада могут достигать 120 мм (длина яйцеклада до 45 мм).

from the poem "Everything about Liza"

KOLYA TELLS THE LIFEGUARD WHAT HE HAS SEEN

I was leading a hike in our local spots
scouts honor and so on
two nights out and I was ready
to throttle those rug rats with my own hands
(I have a solingen see Liza)
squealing and scampering round the pests
while we're in all this ecology and refuge
the *Cecchiniola* leaf beetle's a rare endemic[1]
caddis flies in every creek and Liza that's
an indicator of the absence of pollution
we've got dryads under every bush here
cicadas under every leaf
and no goddamn call to kick up a fuss out here in nature

usually I really don't mind kids
but we got rules here and they're all over the place
and all at once.

    the children say:
    when you come out
    of the water right away
    such heaviness
    such joy
    so much light
    salt on skin
    if this
    isn't heaven then what is

---

1   By the way Liza the biggest cricket in our area of the Orthoptera order, a bush cricket (Saga pedo Pall), reproduces parthenogenetically and no males are found in this territory. The females of this species can reach 120 mm from the head to the end of the ovipositor (the ovipositor can be up to 45 mm long).

*(что с них возьмешь – они же
еще дети)*

встали лагерем в разрешенном месте

это было
типа такое облако с плоским верхом
и заостренным низом в общем похоже
на огромный волчок и оно вращалось
опираясь иглой на воду
я вообще-то такое неоднократно видел
но тут голяк плоскогорье укрыться негде
а у меня на руках пятнадцать мелких уродов
а оно может очень быстро двигаться Лиза

это впрочем продолжало стоять на месте
вращаться

ты в энэло по жизни хоть как-то веришь?

Лиза они забрали всех наших мертвых

там в заливе
если лечь над обрывом и приглядеться
так чтобы не отсвечивала поверхность
в темноте в прохладе
стоят бок о бок

он их вытягивал словно бы пылесосом

так они поднимались ему навстречу
светлым полупрозрачным бесшумным роем
сонмища человеческих коловраток
свет поднимался к свету

(what can you expect of them—they're still
kids)

we set up camp in an authorized area

it was
like a sort of cloud with a flat top
and a pointy bottom really it looked
like a huge top and it was spinning
with its needle resting on the water
actually I've seen something like it more than once
but here was this totally open flatland nowhere to hide
and I've got fifteen little monsters on my hands
and it can move really fast Liza

but anyway it went on standing in place
spinning

do you believe in UFOs even a little?

Liza they took all of our dead

there in the inlet
if you lie down up at the top of the bluff and look carefully
so the surface doesn't reflect light back
in the darkness the cool
they're standing there shoulder to shoulder

it was sucking them up like it was a vacuum

so they were rising up toward it
in a shining half-transparent noiseless swarm
a multitude of human rotifers
light rising toward light

если честно
я не думаю что это были пришельцы
я скорее склонен думать Лиза это
было то что прокл именовал световым телом, иначе говоря,
некое условное обобщение срединной между душой и телом
сущности. При определенных обстоятельствах душа способна
приобретать откуда-то извне огненное или какое-то
воздушное тело. В таком случае это нечто всасывающее души
есть выражение вращающегося в себе умного огня призванного
поместить отделенные от тел совершенно очищенные души в
занебесном согласно версии дамаския месте.
я только не могу понять почему они так долго ждали Лиза
сколько лет они стояли во мгле бок о бок
волны шумели в их черепных коробках
или же времени нету для тех в занебесных сферах

обопрись на меня
поднимайся брат
видишь стоит у врат
обладатель умного огня
постноуменальный инженер
вращающихся сфер

столько влажных лет
ребер рыб темноты
поднимайся я и ты
летим на свет
отворяется коридор
в блистающий мир
где со склона на склон
перелетает в луче
бабочка аполлон
с красным пятном на плече

honestly
I don't think it was aliens
I'm more inclined to think Liza it
was what Proclus referred to as a body of light, in other words, a
sort of notional abstraction of an essence somewhere between the
soul and body. Under certain circumstances the soul is capable of
acquiring from some outside source a fiery or a sort of ethereal
body. In this case this something that sucks in souls is an expression
of an intelligent fire revolving inside of itself meant to place utterly
purified souls separated from bodies into a place according to
Damascius beyond the heavens.
I just can't understand why they waited so long Liza
how many years they stood there in the mist shoulder to shoulder
the waves crashed in their skullboxes
or maybe there's no time for the ones in the heavenly spheres

lean on me
brother get up
see there at the gate
one who bears intelligent fire
a postnoumenal engineer
of the revolving spheres

how many damp years
of ribs of fish of dark
get up you and I
fly toward the light
a corridor is opening
into a radiant world
where from peak to peak
fluttering in a shining beam
the apollo butterfly
red spot on the shoulder

Человечек

Человечек перемещается на восток
У него есть лампочка и свисток,
Если надо, он дернет за два шнурка
И поддует резиновый свой жилет,
Человечек передвигает часы вперед,
Далеко внизу под ногами соленый лед,
Ледяное крошево, стелющаяся мука.
Никому не нужный, маленький и смешной
Человечек перемещается над тишиной,
Над безглазой хлябью, где ни одного огня,
Он умеет дуть в свисток, но тому не рад;
Так висят во тьме человечки, за рядом ряд,
Молчаливый парад, блуждающий вертоград,
Сотня душ, не отличающих ночь от дня.
. . . по воде плывет замороженная вода . . .
Ах, как сладко, когда, вселенную теребя
Бортовыми огнями, ищут во тьме тебя,
Нет честнее дела, чем дуть в свисток, поддувать жилет,
Человечек с тоской прислушивается: вот-вот . . .
Но гудят моторы, в стакане плавится лед,
Стюардесса предлагает курицу на обед,
И надежды нет.

Little Person

A little person's moving toward the east
The person has a whistle and a light,
If called for, there are two strings to release
And the rubber life vest will inflate,
The little person spins clock-arms ahead,
Far down below ice, salt-strewn, lies in shreds,
Spreads out far underfoot, an agonizing state.
Of use to no one, laughable and tiny
The little person's moving over silence,
Above the eyeless ooze, where not a light is lit,
The whistle can be blown, but they're hardly glad of it;
Thus little people in dark suspended, row after row,
A taciturn parade, a gated garden roaming slow,
A hundred souls that know not day from night.
. . . atop the water frozen water floats . . .
Oh, how sweet it is when, with navigation lights
tousling the universe, they seek you in the dark,
No better time to blow the whistle, pump the vest,
The little person, doleful, listens: any minute now . . .
But ice melts in the glass, the motors thunder on,
The stewardess offers chicken breast for lunch,
And hope is gone.

Осень На Большом Фонтане

Перемещение волн, планет,

Тектонических плит

С каждым днем ускоряется.

Из сектора Леонид

Брызжет красно-зеленый свет.

Цикады, сидя лицом к лицу,

Грызут под кустом мацу.

·

В старом пансионате лечебный душ,

Золотой пляж,

По вечерам кино

Про корабль, который унес на дно

Пятнадцать сотен душ,

Но трепещет экранное полотно,

Потому что не так давно

Тетя Лиза тоже ушла на дно

И тетя Фира ушла на дно,

Autumn at the Grand Fountain

The shifting of the planets, waves,

And also the tectonic plates

Is speeding up with every passing day.

From the radiant of Leonid

Dazzling light, a red-green spray.

Cicadas sitting vis-à-vis

Are gnawing matzo 'neath a tree.

•

Therapeutic showers at the old watering hole,

A golden beach,

Films at night

About a ship that sank outright

With fifteen thousand souls,

But the picture quivers, blurs,

For it wasn't very long ago

That Aunt Liza also sank outright

And our Auntie Fira sank outright,

С Ивановыми заодно,

Оттого в соседнем доме темно,

И в старом саду темно,

И блуждает во тьме одинокий луч,

Задевая глазное дно,

И бледная роза *Gloria Dei*

Утратила веру в людей.

•

Улыбнись пошире, садовый клоп,

Подними свой могучий лоб,

Ты похож на трамвай, что бежит домой

Со своей прицепной женой,

Мимо трав и вер и прочих приправ

На любой прихотливый вкус,

На тебя наваливается свод небес,

У тебя обломился ус,

Тяжело бежать, наступает мрак,

Стало очень много больших собак,

Тополь дышит, словно огромный слон,

Bringing Ivanov along for spite,

That's why the neighbor's house is dark at night,

And the ancient garden's dark at night,

And a sole beam blunders in the dark,

Afflicting eyeballs with its light,

And the pale rose *Gloria Dei*

Feels faith in humans slip away.

•

Let's see you smile wider, stink bug

Raise up that mighty mug,

You look like a tram, running home

With wife trailing in tow,

Past the grasses, faiths, and other seasonings

To suit any fastidious taste,

The firmament collapses onto you,

Your whisker torn, defaced,

It's hard to run, the dark is falling,

A gang of large dogs lingers, lolling,

The poplar like an elephant breathes hard,

Поднимаясь на склон.

•

А трамвай несется, разинув рот, —

Он разбойник и соловей,

И когда приближается поворот,

Пассажиры кричат «Ой-вэй!»,

Софа с внуком, Варя совсем одна,

Рабинович, его жена . . .

Им бы всем сойти тыщу лет назад,

А они все сидят.

Проросли их яблоки и айва,

Башмаки оплела трава.

•

Оползающий пласт слоистых пород,

Топология птичьих трасс,

Рыбы, заглатывающие кислород,

Не знают иных таласс,

Жирный ил, копошащаяся слюда,

Пузыри у темного рта,

Climbing up the grassy sward.

•

And the tram speeds on, its mouth agape—

A robber and a nightingale at play,

And when it leans to take a turn,

The passengers cry out "Oy vey!"

Sofa with her grandson, Varya all alone,

Rabinovich and his wife the crone . . .

They should have all got off an age ago,

But they just go on sitting even so.

They've overgrown with quinces and with pears,

The grass has twined itself into their hair.

•

Sliding bed of stratified layers,

Topology of avian traffic,

The fish gulping hungrily for air

Know of no other thalassas,

The bustling mica, oily mire,

Dark mouth blowing bubbles up,

Лебеда, лепечущая вода,

Куриная слепота.

•

Провожая в последний путь

Красные облака,

Приняв на грудь

Пару литров пивка,

Наблюдать водоем,

Заполняющий окоем,

Несравненно лучше,

Если когда вдвоем.

•

А все же оно доводит до слез,

Особенно солнечным днем,

Когда воздух горит с четырех сторон

Синим, что твой купорос,

И пасмурным днем, и вечерним днем,

И ночным медлительным днем,

Когда планеты кружат над ним,

Lamb's quarters, babbling gyre,

Buttercup.

•

Paying last respects

To these crimson clouds,

Having tossed back

A few bottles (but not plowed),

To contemplate this reservoir

That reaches past your stare

Is better by far

When you're there as a pair.

•

But still it can drive you to tears,

Especially on sunny days,

When the air burns bright across the spheres

Blue like that vitriol of yours,

And on overcast days, and evening days,

And slow-moving nighttime days,

When the planets circle it in thrall,

Как рой золотистых ос,

Поэтому лучше теперь и впредь

Туда вообще не смотреть.

•

Две недели есть у меня,

У меня есть четыре дня,

У меня есть пара часов,

А потом уже нет ничего...

•

Вырой мне норку, жук,

Лапками шевеля,

Я еще полежу,

Теплая, как земля . . .

Что она говорит,

Выплыв из темноты,

Бабка со связкой рыб,

Разевающих рты?

Like gold-gleaming wasps out from the nest,

That's why from here on out you'd best

Not look over there at all.

•

Two weeks I've got,

I've got four days,

I've got a couple hours,

And then nothing anymore . . .

•

Beetle, dig me out a burrow,

Wiggle those legs back and forth,

I'll lie here a bit longer,

Warm as the earth . . .

What's that she's calling out,

From the darkness taking shape,

That woman with her string of trout,

Their mouths agape?

Ночью не спится но утром есть чем заняться
В облачном небе луна бежит как волчица
После определенного возраста перестаешь бояться
Потому что ничего с тобой уже не может случиться
Разве что при неловком движении о себе напомнит ключица
Потом приходится долго лечиться
И нельзя наклоняться

Над порогом прибита подкова от сглаза
В саду мальвы за плетнем спуск к речке
Там на берегу играют в войну маленькие человечки
Из которых каждый убит не по одному разу
Но встает стряхивает песчинки
Забирает свои машинки
Правда с каждым разом все трудней подниматься

За рекою ночами слышны взрывы
Там в три смены добывают в карьерах кровавик-камень
Не иначе хотят перевыполнить план добычи
Оттого и эти сухие грозы эти зарницы в полнеба
Оттого заснуть и не удается
Да к тому же скрипят половицы в пустом доме
Кто-то ходит по ним
Кто то ходит
Кого не видно

from FOUR SEASONED YEARS OF TIME

Can't sleep at night but plenty to do in the morning
Moon in the cloudy sky running like a she-wolf
After a certain age you stop being scared
Because nothing can happen to you anymore
Except maybe when you move wrong and your collarbone complains
Afterward it takes a long time to heal
And you can't bend over anymore

Horseshoe over the threshold against the evil eye
Hollyhocks in the garden, out the fence down to the creek
There the little people play war on the banks
Each one of them killed and not for the first time
But they get up shake off the sand
Gather up their little trucks
Though every time it gets harder to get up

On the far bank explosions roar by night
Three shifts a day mine the quarries for bloodstone
Must be trying to overreach the target yield
That's where we get these dry thunderstorms these half-sky dawns
That's why we can't fall asleep
And on top of that the floorboards creak in this empty house
Someone's walking on them
Someone's walking
Who can't be seen

Maria Galina & Ainsley Morse
Talk Translation

AM: When you were choosing poems for me to translate, did you think about their translatability?

MG: Unfortunately, I did. I was cravenly combing through the overall mass for texts that would be guaranteed to make their way to readers with nothing lost. This may be a mistake—for me and for others—the idea that you should undertake tasks within the boundaries of the possible. You might detect some hidden authorial arrogance in the attempt to seek out texts that are easier to translate (and thus easier to understand). But you might also see arrogance in an author's having no mercy for the translator, not even thinking about how much effort, time, and energy she has to spend in producing a decent translation of a formally complex text. And meanwhile that particular text might not even be worth it. So I am most pleased when the translator chooses the texts on her own. At least then it's all being done for love—and the author relinquishes both responsibility and guilt.

AM: Do you ever think about how your texts (or even phrases/ certain parts) might sound in English?

MG: No. I exist permanently inside of language. Although I do have translations I've done into English. But that's a whole different area, the hatch closes and the translated texts stay there, behind the hatch. I don't think about them. A text is also the physical substance of the language; you can tear it off, of course, but it'll hurt. And it's the sound, and the meanings that appear unexpectedly when you stick two words together.

The funniest thing is that I sometimes recite memorized English-language texts to myself, but since I'm an amateur, it's a strange mix. Like, I'm always remembering Jane Ingelow's "Methought the stars were blinking bright / And the old brig's sails unfurl'd . . .," mostly thanks to Agatha Christie, since I first read the lines in one of her novels. And I'm utterly enchanted by Wordsworth's "Lucy." But [lines/poems like these] are not connected with what I do on my own; I need them for finding harmony in the world, maybe.

AM: Has your translation practice ever affected your own Russian-language texts?

MG: I don't think so. For me these are different, almost completely discrete areas, though I think I probably lose a lot by not letting other rhythms and poetic tool kits into my texts. Or maybe I do let them in without noticing it? I'm not sure. I've worked with texts that seem to have just independently recalibrated themselves in Russian, like Carol Ann Duffy's "Nile"—even the sound patterning stayed intact. Or Dorothy Parker's "Salome's Dancing-Lesson," which I translated for pure personal pleasure, daring myself to see if I could do it. But I spent several months on a poem by Fiona Sampson, rewriting each line ten times or more. Even as I understood everything perfectly on a human level. The experience of translating is good in and of itself, since it unshackles you, loosens you up, but not much more. Generally you end up translating either what seems close and familiar to you or what seems like a challenge; completely different approaches, but they both work.

AM: In the poems of yours I've translated, which words, phrases, or other formal elements strike you as the most difficult to translate?

MG: Slang and the combination of different lexical layers (registers). Certain very specific local details, Soviet stuff. The sounds. Like, in the excerpt from "Everything about Liza," the z sound runs through the whole text; it just somehow turned out like that, but since it did, it's probably important.

It's hard with memes, jokes that Russian readers get and take in stride but English-language readers utterly miss. Like the word *medved* that I have in one of my poems, which refers to an old Runet joke and the made-up "Olbanian" language. And that's not to mention hidden quotations—contemporary Russian poems often refer to other contemporary Russian poems; the Russian reader may be able to decipher the reference but it's not like we expect English-language readers to know all of Russian poetry . . .

AM: What do you think about "versions," "free translations"? And when thinking about what is "lost in translation," what do you most fear losing?

MG: Translation is always a compromise, you have to decide each time what to leave and what to throw overboard to keep this hot-air balloon afloat. Sometimes a free translation works better than a literal one, like with Grigory Dashevsky's translations of Catullus. On the other hand [Samuil] Marshak translated [Robert Louis] Stevenson's "Heather Ale" such that it's exactly the same text from top to bottom, like it's not in a different language. I've had fantastic luck with translators; when Sasha Dugdale translated some of my poems, it was a perfect match.

The same problems crop up, surprisingly, even with closely related languages, like Ukrainian. When you're thinking about what is or isn't translatable you can see to what extent it's a different culture with different traditions—linguistic, psychological. A few of my poems were translated by Marianna Kiyanovskaya, a marvelous [Ukrainian] poet and translator, and yes, it's a free translation and yes, it's a precise text—seems like a paradox but in fact it just works like that.

A text is not meaning and not rhythm, and not sound, and not details, it's all of that taken together plus some kind of cultural background, hidden quotations that, willy-nilly, nearly everybody is carrying around. Something will inevitably be lost, so let it be the cultural background. I wouldn't want to lose the sound, and the meaning is what comes across on its own, as long as the sounds are right.

Now some questions for you: what was easiest and hardest for you while working with these texts?

AM: The easiest part was probably, to borrow your phrase, "understanding everything perfectly on a human level." I "heard" the poems in a very unmediated way, and sometimes it seemed like they'd gone straight into English in my head and all I had to do was write them down "on paper"/type them up. You saw the first drafts—they weren't bad. But then I decided I needed more rhyme, that it was a really important part of your poetics. When I read and listened more deeply I felt that the poems were, on the one hand, narrative—they have plots—but meanwhile the rhymes seem to participate in this narrative quality, they provide a sort of skaz and a meta-layer, like a second narrator. And I really wanted to get that across. Though at the same time I think the character of your rhyming is very Russian, or Soviet/post-Soviet, and that simply reproducing the rhymes will hardly give English-language readers a real understanding of this characteristic intonation. So I was beating my head against the wall, trying to translate with rhyme while feeling not at all sure it would pay off. I'm afraid I may have been possessed by a kind of mania to "rhyme at all costs," while some of the poems work fine in English without rhyme (like most of "Everything about Liza," although I really like that poem's combination of unobtrusive rhyme and prose fragments).

MG: To English-language readers, how familiar and comprehensible is Russian—not poetry per se, but the network of images and ideas that contemporary Russian authors refer to? Who are the readers of Russian poetry in English translation?

University students or professors of the humanities? Does anyone outside of the academy read this stuff?

AM: Even though you asked these as separate questions I think they have common answers. In my opinion there's a big difference between Russian and American readers of poetry—partly a blunt difference in numbers (I think there are objectively fewer poetry readers in the US), but it has to do with different reading cultures. If you're talking about readers of more experimental contemporary poetry, maybe the numbers are similar; but in Russia there is still just a much larger contingent of people who read poetry *voobshche* [in general]. And there's a stable canon of classical poetry that is still part of school curricula, perceived as an important element of cultural heritage. So besides the difference in numbers there's a different level of familiarity with poetry as an existing and relevant genre—that works with the network of images and ideas you refer to. English-language readers who didn't study Russian literature in college don't participate in that familiarity, they won't pick up a subtle Mandelstam or Tsvetaeva reference (let alone Derzhavin).

Even in universities many people don't teach poetry in translation, because they think poetry can't be translated or that students won't know what to do with it. In my experience students like poetry—many of them write poems—but they have a hard time reading, analyzing, or discussing poems in a nonsuperficial way; it's a skill they haven't been taught. And since there are few (or only bad) translations of nineteenth-century Russian poetry, we end up teaching twentieth- (or twenty-first)-century poetry in a vacuum— even in the academic setting we have a hard time establishing that network of images and ideas. Everyone gets it when Prigov name-checks Stalin, but anything more subtle than that is going to go unnoticed by most readers. But then it's interesting to see newer Russian poetry that's more "transparent," with more overt allusions that are also less tied to a specifically Russian/Soviet historical-literary context; these differences make it simultaneously more and less satisfying to translate, you can be more confident about getting things across while also feeling like you're getting off easy.

Still, there are definitely nonacademic readers of Russian poetry in translation. The Russian American literary communities have the best of both worlds (some frame of Russian cultural reference plus fluency in American culture). And there are English-language poets (and other readers) who find things in translated poetry that we translators don't even notice. These are my favorite readers, really, the ones who inspire me to keep translating.

Poems by Aleksandra Tsibulia

TRANSLATED BY CATHERINE CIEPIELA

ALEKSANDRA TSIBULIA is a poet and literary critic. A resident of Saint Petersburg, she currently works at the State Hermitage Museum. In 2014, after winning the Russian Gulliver Prize, she published *Puteshestvie na Krai Krovi* (*Journey to the Edge of Blood*) and in 2015 won the Arkady Dragomoshchenko Award for young Russophone poets. Her new book, titled *Koleso Obozreniya* (*The Ferris Wheel*), is available from Jaromír Hladík press. She has participated in the Runokuu Poetry Festival in Helsinki (2015), the sound art and video art festival Poetronics in Moscow, and the Seoul International Writers' Festival (2019), among other events. Her poetry has been translated into English, Italian, Korean, Swedish, and Finnish.

CATHERINE CIEPIELA is a scholar and translator of Russian poetry who teaches at Amherst College. She is the author of a book on Marina Tsvetaeva and Boris Pasternak, as well as coeditor, with Honor Moore, of the anthology *The Stray Dog Cabaret*. Ciepiela is also editor of *Relocations: Three Contemporary Russian Women Poets*. Her translations have appeared in *The Nation*, *The Massachusetts Review*, *Seneca Review*, *The Common*, *Pequod*, and elsewhere. Her translation of Polina Barskova's book of poetic essays will be published next year with New York Review Books.

Есть время для мира, оно очень короткое,
выпрошенная у гордости и судьбы
«ночь любви в меланхоличном Аиде».
Есть время для трепета, когда я нахожу
твою ресницу между страниц
ненадолго одолженной книги.
Есть только-наш-жест, пропущенный через стыд,
который удалось залечить и вернуть себе.
Есть час, когда меня почти отбрасывает волна сияния,
бьющая прямо в висок из твоей груди,
от тела, покоящегося, возможно, совсем не здесь,
возможно, в мечтах о «пустой глазнице».

There's time for peace, a brief time,
"a night of love in melancholy Hades"
granted by pride and fate.
There's time for a shiver when I find
your eyelash stuck between the pages of
a book loaned for a little while.
There's the ours-only gesture, filtered through shame,
which we managed to heal and bring back.
There's the hour when I'm nearly capsized by the wave of light
beaming straight at my temple from your chest,
from the body that reposes, possibly somewhere else entirely,
possibly in dreams about a "hollow eye socket."

Пожалуй, первый теплый вечер за последнее время. Я намеренно иду той же дорогой, что и после взрыва, через два моста. Людей не меньше, но теперь они выглядят расслабленно, видно, что они «прогуливаются»; их никто не неволит, спешившись, преодолевать непредвиденные расстояния. Повсеместно присутствуют так называемые влюбленные. Они облепили также и фонтаны, которые в отсутствие воды напоминают какие-то мемориальные монументы. Из находок — оттаявшая снежинка из фольги. Кто-то произносит «чморили», затем — «шикардос». Между минаретов мечети появляется полная луна, она приобретает форму ясности. Теперь кажется, что все уже решено. И я тоже праздную: скупое, невзрачное возвращение (надолго отступившей) речи.

It's maybe the first warm evening we've had lately. I deliberately take the same route I took after the explosion, across two bridges. There are just as many people, but this time they look relaxed, obviously just "taking a stroll"; no one's forcing them, after dismounting, to cover unexpected distances. The place is filled with so-called lovers. They're crowded onto the fountains, which, in the absence of water, resemble some kind of commemorative monuments. One of my finds—a melted snowflake made of foil. Someone says "got shafted," then "totally fab." Through the mosque's minarets a full moon rises, takes the shape of clarity. Looks like it's all settled now. And I'm also celebrating: the meager, nondescript return (after a long retreat) of speech.

С колеса обозрения видно, что наступила осень:
красные и желтые деревья, люди
летают на ракете посреди грусти. Бездомные,
как космонавты в космосе: никогда не будут
похоронены, так и будут дрейфовать или сгорят
среди звезд. Тихие животные нежно лижут
кожу и шерсть, на Земле.

From the Ferris wheel you can see autumn is here:
red and yellow trees, people flying on a rocket
inside the sadness. They're homeless,
like cosmonauts in the cosmos, who never
get buried, so they drift or burn up
among the stars. Placid animals gently groom
flesh and fur, back on Earth.

Непрерывно сменяющиеся дистанции,
самые непроходимые из которых невидимые.
Непрозрачность вещей, потому что прозрачны
только мертвые вещи, ставшие некрасивыми призраками.
Неоткрытые вещи и их сопротивление силам зрения:
созревая, они оборачиваются подарками.
Компрессия траекторий и правил
игры, повиснувших в невесомости,
они, в конце концов, и определяют контуры
этого слова, запрещенного к произнесению.

Distances continually being replaced,
the most impassable of which are invisible.
The opaqueness of things, since only dead things
are transparent, having become unsightly ghosts.
Unopen things and their resistance to powers of vision:
ripening, they're transformed into gifts.
The compression of the game's trajectories
and rules, suspended in weightlessness,
these, in the end, determine the contours
of this word, which it is forbidden to pronounce.

Пару минут
длится в пространстве любимое тело
в виде молний, зигзагов и легких пружин.
Взгляд А и взгляд В
преобразуются в воздухе в знак «равно».
Он так и висит над всем залом,
пока сами они
становятся невидимыми.

For a couple of minutes
a loved body lengthens in space
in the form of lightning flashes, zigzags, and weightless springs.
Gaze A and gaze B
change in the air into an equal sign.
There it hangs above the entire hall,
as they themselves
turn invisible.

Как известно, белки, как дети из детского дома, никогда не отказываются от еды: они помещают орешки в неглубокие лунки, к которым никогда не вернутся.

Говорят, забывчивые белки не в силах отыскать припрятанные ресурсы, они запасаются безоглядно, в свободном дарении умножая тайники непреднамеренной щедрости.

Я вижу товарищество деловитых белок-беглянок, зарывающих плоды неотчужденного труда в землю, как маленьких Йозефов Бойсов, с будущими дубами.

It's well known that squirrels, like children from the orphanage, never turn down food: they hide nuts in shallow holes and never go back for them.

It's said these forgetful squirrels aren't capable of looking for their hidden stores, that they save things recklessly, multiplying their caches of unpremeditated generosity in a free act of giving.

I see the comradeship of diligent squirrel-fugitives, burying the fruits of their unalienated labor in the ground like tiny Joseph Beuyses with their future oaks.

Сбиты балконы с балясинами на Липовой, что означает
уже необратимое крушение: конец
этой затянувшейся связи и самонаказания.
Деревья, собравшиеся как друиды, рогатины
тополей, брандмауэры. Другие места,
маркированные как боль. Лупоглазые саженцы ивы
(некоторые из них до сих пор спеленаты),
чье мистическое свечение нельзя отрицать.
Небо стянуто в одну точку и расположено
полосками. Земля надорвана,
пережившая ампутацию человека.

The balconies with balusters on Lipovaya are broken, signaling
irreversible collapse: an end
to this prolonged relation and self-punishment.
Trees gathered like druids, bear-spears of poplars,
firewalls. Other places, as locatable
as pain. Pop-eyed willow saplings
(some wrapped in canvas, even now),
whose mystical fluorescence can't be denied.
Sky twisted to a single point and arranged
in stripes. Earth torn open
after the amputation of man.

Выпадение из поля внимания. Выскользнувший, ненаходимый внутри момент необратимости, на отрезке с сентября по январь. Длительность, в течение которой ты обнимаешь незнакомую мне девушку у стойки бара. Все это время я как будто нахожусь под водой. Пластинка, которая приятно шуршит. Белые брюки. «Петербургский текст» Малой Коломны. Верфи, за которыми как будто бы все заканчивается, возможно, это и есть тот самый «экзистенциальный горизонт»? Если обогнуть верфи, то окажешься там, где следует оказаться, то есть с двумя мужиками и стиральной машиной посреди Псковской улицы. Вечер, но еще не стемнело. Снег мелкий и сухой, как порошок.

Gone from the field of attention. Lost, unfindable inside, that turning point in the interval between September and January. That duration of time in the course of which you caress a girl I don't know seated at the bar. The whole while it's like I'm underwater. A record playing with a pleasing hiss. White trousers. "The Petersburg text" of Little Kolomna. Shipyards behind which earth seems to reach its end. Could this be that very same "existential horizon"? If you bend the shipyards, you'll end up where you should be, that is, with two guys and a washing machine in the middle of Pskovskaya Street. It's evening, but not dark yet. The snow is fine and dry, like powder.

Catherine Ciepiela & Aleksandra Tsibulia, in Conversation

CC: I find that a real challenge for the translator is allowing the poem to keep its secrets. I try to let my translations offer up the mysteries of the original. But those mysteries were "made," as the Russian formalists would say, by the poet, and the translator needs to understand how they were made. Somehow she must possess this understanding but withhold it in her translation.

With your poems, especially, I feel it's important to honor their reticence. When I was working on "There's time, a short one, for peace," you shared with me the circumstance that helped shape the poem: a painful break with a lover that was enacted by an "ours-only gesture." During our workshop, my fellow translators wanted to know what the gesture was. I understood their curiosity as the translator's need to know in order to do the work (though perhaps our interest is prurient).

How do you think about this matter of how poetry like your own can be catalyzed by experience but move beyond it?

AT: In one of my poems I wrote, "I no longer think poetry must be opaque,/ it must be austere and confiding." What's important to me is the inner fire and agitation, the nakedness and exposure of the speaker, her openness, and not outright erotics. I'm sympathetic to the idea of poetry as experience, but more in the sense of interior micro-events, movements occurring in small worlds, extreme states, irretrievable objects, experience on a level with the mystical and religious: enchantment, possession, epiphanies, things that evoke a cathartic feeling (or a feeling of endless despair).

It's important not to scare off life's tenderness and its faint pulsing. How do you speak about what's miraculous or piercing, about the unspoken, about the kind of grief language retreats before? It took me five years to write about the death of someone I was close to, but suddenly, during an illness, the intonation appeared as I was reading Tor Ulven, and I was able to tell in poetry the story I couldn't tell out loud all those years. It wasn't a story about horror and fear but about sharing a tender look and final touch with a precious being.

CC: What I just called the reticence of your writing seems like both a cause and effect of your form. Your poems are loaded with meaning and experience, but they are brief and spare. When translating you, I felt charged to give each word the same weight, meaning that the stakes are high for every word choice. In the same poem, "There's time, a short one, for peace," we lingered over how to translate "trepet'," whose dictionary meaning is "tremble." You explained that the sensation had a mystical, erotic tinge, and "tremble" seemed too virginal, too nineteenth-century. I went with "shiver," a quick jolt to the nerves.

When you compose, do you deliberate over each word, or do they come in a string, in a sequence? Do you have the same sense that each word matters?

AT: Usually I write poetic texts in one sitting (an evening) and don't rework them afterward. (I know Arkady Dragomoshchenko and his followers would endlessly rewrite their texts, going back to them again and again, making them more concentrated and intense.)

Poems appear to me like objects, crystals, where, yes, each word needs to be in its proper place, but word choice is less important to me than intonation, because you can't fake an intonation, and that's the most important thing in a poem. I don't write "in books," I don't think in big projects; I write discrete texts, and it's important to me that they "catch fire" quickly and come into being on their own.

Sometimes (as in the poem you cite) someone else's speech appears, as a sort of incrustation—the speech of someone I'm close to or a lover, words I've carried inside myself for a long time, or a quotation from another poet I'm "winking" at across time, or just a phrase heard on the street, which can offer no less powerful illumination. Something happens, and these elements coincide, rhyme, cohere.

CC: Our selection includes both your verse and prose poems. The prose poem hasn't been strongly developed in Russian poetry. The first noteworthy example was provided by Ivan Turgenev, whose Frenchness may account for his interest in the form. I'm interested in how you started working in this form, which makes different demands on the translator. With the prose poems, I'm gratefully freed from choosing line endings and can concentrate on syntactical rhythm.

AT: As we know, prose also has its rhythms, but they are more complicated than in poetry. The text itself usually decides what it wants: whether to be divided into lines or not. In principle, I don't see any special difference; the main thing, again, is the intonation and kind of breathing you choose, and how, precisely here, the line needs to unfold.

I started writing prose poems quite a while ago, but it was most likely the influence of foreign literature. Tomas Tranströmer, Unica Zürn, Robert Walser. And in my school years, Baudelaire and other French writers.

CC: Did you understand anything new about your poems from the experience of being translated? I remember you were surprised, when I pointed it out, to learn that you used the negative prefix "не" so often in your wonderful poem, "Constantly shifting distances" (a line which contains a negative prefix I failed to capture!).

AT: For me, this experience of collaborative work was very important; sometimes it was awkward to have to "undo the spell" of your own poetic texts and talk about what lies behind this or that image or word so you can choose an equivalent in another language. It's like having to explain a joke or paraphrase a poem. It's such a magical practice: first you pour in dead water, then living water. You have to kill the poem, reassemble it, and cast a new spell in order to reinvent it by means of another language.

Poems by Oksana Vasyakina

Translated by Anna Halberstadt

Oksana Vasyakina is a poet, writer, feminist activist, and curator of creative writing courses. She was born in 1989 in Ust-Ilimsk (Irkutsk Oblast) and graduated from the Maxim Gorky Literature Institute and the School of Performance Pyrfyr. She has received numerous literary awards and her debut book, *Women's Prose*, was shortlisted for the Andrei Bely Prize in 2016. Her book *Wind of Fury* was published by AST, the largest book house in Russia. In 2021, her debut novel *The Wound* was published by *New Literary Review*. Vasyakina's poems have been translated into Italian, English, and Estonian. She lives and works in Moscow.

Anna Halberstadt is a poet, translator, and clinical psychologist who grew up in Lithuania. She has published numerous collections of poetry in English (including *Vilnius Diary* and *Green in a Landscape with Ashes*) and in Russian (*Transit* and *Gloomy Sun*). She has translated poetry by Eileen Myles, Edward Hirsch, and Bob Dylan, among others, and has received many awards for her writing and translations, including 2017 Translator of the Year from *Persona PLUS journal* for her translation of Bob Dylan's poem "Brownsville Girl." The Lithuanian Translators Association included *Vilnius Diary* on its list of most important books in translation in 2017, and *Lt.15* named her new book of selected poems in Lithuanian translation, *Transit*, one of the top fifteen poetry books of 2020.

Теория Блика

α

Опыт близок блику
Близок местоимению твой – стертое слово пустое как
     жестяная ржавая банка –
И я пишу *твой затылок с дорожкой темных крапинок*
     родимого пятна
Твой приближает меня к твоей коже
И я очень близко смотрю в *твой затылок*
И могу почувствовать как пахнет кожа и через вдох стать
     продолжением *твоего тела*

Я – *тело твое*
Я *телом твой взгляд* ощущаю
И прикасаясь к тебе *твою ощущаю отдачу*
Как будто ты камень ночной хранящий тепло заката
Опыт сбивается в быстрый неуловимый скачок
И я стараюсь его о/ухватить развернуть его
И воображаю что это возможно – вот так в темноте
     рассматривая светлые пятна
Отпечатки на стенах книжных полках и потолке –
Ускользающий блик распечатать.

β

Пишу *лесбийский*
Язык утопает в теле
Знак блекнет на коже
Как *твой* опустошаются имена
Имена как капельки холодной слюны разлетаются и исчезают
Пишу блик
Теорию блика

Theory of Glare

α

Experience is close to a glare
Close to the pronoun your—an erased word, empty like a rusty tin
    can—
And I am writing *the back of your head with the trail of dark specks*
    of a birthmark
Your gets me near *your skin*
And I am very close to you, staring at *the back of your head*
And I can feel how your skin smells and through my inhale I
    become an extension of your body

I am *your body*
I feel *your gaze* with my body
And when touching you, *I feel you recoil*
As if you were a stone in the night that preserved the warmth of a
    sunset
Experience turns into a fast elusive leap
And I try to grab/embrace and unfold it
And I imagine it's possible—just like this, just so, looking at bright
    spots in the dark
Imprints on the walls, bookshelves, and the ceiling—
To print this elusive glare.

β

I write *lesbian*
Tongue drowns in the body
A sign pales on the skin
Names get emptied like *your*
Names, like droplets of cold saliva, fly off and disappear
I write *glare*
Theory of glare

γ

Отпечаток блика замкнут
Он означает самого себя и сам себя повторяет он сам себе
     зеркало и тело в нем самом отраженное
И трепет блика
Прожигает пространство
Темнота остается

δ

Твои твой твоя твою твоего тебя
Рассматриваю тело твое великое и вижу кисти рук твоих
     великих и дальше – плечи тяжелые от величины
Но проброситься дальше
Проброситься взглядом в простирающееся время жизни

Здесь печать
Отпечаток блика

ε

Мой вопрос рождается здесь на пороге печати
Если блик по природе – отголосок света
То его отпечатками будут ожоги
Или плоть зараженная
И он материален.

ζ

Я сижу у тебя на коленях и болтаю ногами шею твою захватив
     и ладонью глажу по мягкому упругому уху
Я сливаюсь с тобой

γ

The print of glare is closed up
It means itself and it repeats itself, it is its own mirror and a body
Reflected in it
And a trembling glare
Burns through space
And the darkness remains

δ

Your your your you your you
I look at your grand body, and I see your grand wrists and farther—
     your shoulders
Heavy from your size
But to throw oneself farther
To throw a glance into the time of our lives, stretched before us

There is a print there
Print of a glare

ε

My question arises here at the threshold of a print
If a glare, by nature, is light's echo
Then its imprints would be burns
Or infected flesh
And it is material.

ζ

I sit on your lap, my legs dangling,
embracing your neck, and I stroke your soft resilient ear
I merge with you

η

Ты вкладываешь пальцы в мой мокрый рот
И я чувствую их солоноватый вкус
И языком провожу по рельефу он твердый как плотный картон
От тебя пахнет бумагой
От тебя пахнет книгой
Ты – книга и мой взгляд скользит по тебе
И между нами смыслы клубятся это мы их образуем
Они красные теплые огненные
Мы образуем смысл

θ

Толчок   Толчок Толчок Толчок
И треском я откликаюсь
Внизу моего живота треск
И между нами звук
Так разрывается тяжелое полотно

ι

Ты тянешь меня
И тянешь меня своим темно-коричневым взглядом
Ты вся гнедая и мной обладаешь
Упругая и изгиб руки бликует в свете желтого торшера

κ

Этот свет приходит сюда промеж нас
Он твердый как газ или пыль
Он твердый как бежевая бумага
На которой пишу *лесбийский*

η

you insert your fingers into my wet mouth
I feel their salty taste
And I feel the relief with my tongue, it is hard like dense cardboard
You smell like paper
You smell like a book
You are a book, and my gaze glides over you
And meanings swirl between us, we develop them
They are red warm fiery
We develop a meaning

θ

A push A push A push A push
And I respond with a crack
A crack under my belly
And a sound between us
That's how a heavy canvas gets torn

ι

You pull me
You pull me with your dark brown gaze
You are a bay mare and you possess me
Supple, and the curve of your arm glares in the light of a yellow
    floor lamp

κ

This light comes here between us
It is hard like gas or dust
It is hard like beige paper
On which I write *lesbian*

λ

Здесь в этом свете и звуке ты мной обладаешь
И я тебе отдаюсь
Как лепесток отдается теченью
Я пишу *лепесток* и *теченье* но мне ближе другое
Я обожаю наш секс
И я люблю слово *трахать*
Я люблю
Когда ты трахаешь меня

Потому что когда ты вставляешь в меня свою руку я
      становлюсь реальной
Когда ты взглядом пришпориваешь меня к подушке
Я узнаю свое тело
Оно белое с пухлыми сияющими грудями
И крохотные соски набухают
Я становлюсь огромной
И готова вмещать тебя всю
Вмещать тебя всю бесконечно

μ

Твой рот раскрыт мне навстречу
Я вижу белесую сухость на изгибе губы
Ты дышишь рычишь
И пахнешь сильнее   сильнее
Пахнешь собой

ν

Ты толкаешь в мой рот свой теплый твердый язык
И я его принимаю

λ

here in this light and this sound you possess me
and I give myself to you
like a petal gives itself to a stream
I write *petal* and *stream*, but I prefer other things
I adore our sex
And I love the word *fuck*
I love
When you fuck me

Because when you insert your hand in me, I turn real
When your gaze spurs me toward the pillow
I learn about my body
It's white with plump shiny breasts
And my tiny nipples swell
I turn huge
I am ready to take in all of you
Keep taking in all of you for the rest of the time

μ

Your mouth opens to greet me
I see the curve of your lip, whitish and dry
You breathe and you growl
And you smell stronger and stronger
Smell like yourself

ν

You push your warm hard tongue into my mouth
And I receive it

ξ

Я вся – твоя влага
Я вся твое влажное место

Твое влажное место

Толчок

о

Я твой взгляд назову
Он имеет меня

π

А я вижу тебя
Ты вся гнедая
Вся превращаешься в силу
И острые груди твои
Так красивы между смуглых расправленных плеч

Р

Я глажу ладонью от уха к щеке к подбородку
И любуюсь твоей головой
Надо мной она так маскулинна
Все тяжелей
Все любимей

σ

Ты меня кормишь собой
Ты меня наполняешь

ξ

All of me—your moisture
All of me—your wet place

Your wet place

A push

o

I will name your gaze
It possesses me

π

And I see you
You are a bay mare
You turn into a force
And your sharp breasts
Are so beautiful between dark spread shoulders

P

I stroke with my palm the space between your ear and cheek and
    your chin
I admire your head
It is so masculine above me
Getting heavier
Becoming beloved

σ

You feed me with your body
You fill me

τ

Голова твоя темнеет между белых моих грудей
И кисти твои темнеют на моих белоснежных боках

υ

Ты дышишь рычишь и вульва моя превращается
В белое льющееся кольцо теплой плоти
Я тебя ей обнимаю и принимаю

φ

Все происходит
Мы происходим
Мы здесь происходим
Мы делаем это вместе

χ

Блик медовый на твоей щеке
Я пальцами прикасаюсь к твоей вульве
Она в руках моих твердеет и вздымается как огонь

ψ

Ты кончаешь исторгая рык становишься больше темнее
Я кончаю раскрыв себя до предела и застывши в дуге

ω

Блик распечатан
Блик распечатан

τ

Your head is so dark between my white breasts
And your wrists are dark on my snow-white sides

υ

you breathe, growl and my vulva turns
into a white pouring ring of warm flesh
I embrace you with it, and I take you in

φ

Everything is happening
We are happening
We are happening here
We are doing it together

χ

A honey-colored glare on your cheek
I touch your vulva with my fingers
It's getting hard, and it rises like a fire

ψ

You come, releasing a growl, you get bigger and darker
I come, opening myself to the limit, freeze in a bridge

ω

Glare got printed
Glare got printed

Опера-балет Гомофобия

утопия – мертвая точка черная на воротничке неопрятной
   рубашки

здесь черным по черному пишет военная форма в холле
   магнитном метро
здесь черным по черному пишет мутный ослепший рассвет
чего тебе хочется? злой победы? или просто идти и дышать
не смрадом дышать не пыль вдыхать не поглощать упадок
но идти и идти как будто идешь и притяженье – это приятное
   обстоятельство тел
кто эти девушки с бритыми головами и одеждой с мужского
   плеча
кто этот парень с длинными подкрашенными у корней
   волосами
ему тесно и в школе его называли пидором и девчонкой но он
   хотел красивые волосы
а еще – немного любви старшеклассника
кто эти девчонки они целуют друг друга в школе их называли
   лесбухами и мужиками
и глаза у них были красные от ночных переписок
они хотят отомстить

утопия – нежный лепесток на жирных рельсах метро в рывках
   воздуха бьется
черным черно пишут каучуковые подошвы черных людей
это взрыв это остановка сердечной мышцы или любовь?
утопия нежная лапка шерстяная
человеческое тело дрожащими линиями распято
каждая выдвигается за границу тебя и что ты там видишь? что
   ты делаешь?
сосешь хуй подрачивая себя?
облизываешь анус любимого тела израненного чужими
   взглядами?

OPERA-BALLET HOMOPHOBIA

utopia—a dead-end black dot on the collar of an unkempt shirt

here black-on-black is the writing of a military uniform in the hall
    of a magnetic metro
here black-on-black is the writing of a cloudy blind sunrise
what do you want? a mean victory? or just to walk and breathe
not to inhale stench, not to inhale dust, not to consume decay
but just walk and walk like you're walking, and attraction—a
    pleasant quality of bodies
who are these girls with shaved heads and clothes taken off a man's
    back
who is this guy with long hair dyed at the roots
he feels constricted and they called him a faggot in school and a girl
but he wanted beautiful hair
and also—just a little—to be loved by a guy from a higher grade
who are these girls they kiss each other in school they were called
    lesbos and dudes
their eyelids were red from corresponding at night
they want revenge

utopia—a tender petal on greasy metro rails pulses in gusts of air
black-on-black is the writing of the vulcanized rubber soles of
    people in black
this explosion—the heart muscle halting, or is it love?
utopia, a tender woolen paw
a man's body crucified by quivering lines
each one of them is moving over the border of you, and what do
    you see there?
what do you do?
suck on the prick while masturbating a little
lick the anus of the beloved body, wounded by strangers' glances?
or separate the vulva's folds?
or are your fingers stems of erotic tentacles threaded

или раздвигаешь складочки вульвы?
или пальцы твои – стебельки эротических щупалец
    проброшенные между камнями скалистого бытия?
или поле широкое это всего лишь бедро лошади пегой?
тебя до тела свели до хуя до пизды до пересечений этих
    органов тела
до голых сосков ненастно покрытых гусиной кожей
до ануса красного свели
а теперь ты лежишь на каменных глыбах брусчатки
вся голая или голый или голое или голые
и ласковый снежок превращается в капли на горячей коже твоей

и перемешивается с солью
с солью московской с солью твоего пота с жирной волною
    секреций
зачем ты лежишь? ты мертвая собака на дороге
еще теплая и шматки алых внутренностей пар отдают в
    декабрьский воздух мясной

и снежок кружится хрупкий
как нежный искалеченный кристалл
и тело твое как в шкатулке
в себя в свою мякоть отверженную принимает холодную сталь

так кружится снежок как утопия ясный
утопия – мертвая точка
линия утопии скорректирована стерильным ножом

это взрыв
или греческий хор
это взрыв или крик человеческого животного дикого
это крик боли
это крик скорректированный и ослабший
это вопль гиены
нет это взрыв утопии черной
засвеченный и погашенный соляризацией

among stones of your rocky being?
or is a wide field only a palomino's hip?
you were reduced to your body your prick your cunt to these
    organs of the body crossing
to naked nipples hungrily covered with goosebumps
reduced to a red anus
and now you are lying on big rough cobblestones
all naked, she-naked, he-naked, they-naked, them-naked
and tender snow melts into droplets on your hot skin

and gets mixed with salt
with Moscow salt with the salt of your perspiration with the oily
    wave of your secretions
why do you lie there? You are a dead dog on the road
still warm and shreds of your scarlet innards are steaming in the
    meaty December air

and fragile snow spins
like a tender mutilated crystal
and your body, like in a jewelry box
takes into itself, into its spurned flesh—cold steel.

thus, snow revolves clear like utopia
utopia—a dead end
utopia's line corrected with a sterile knife

it's an explosion
or a Greek choir
it's an explosion or a scream of a human wild animal
it's a scream of pain
it's a corrected and weakened scream
and hyena's howl
no, it's an explosion of black utopia
burned out and extinguished by solarization

это победа спокойного живота
я наблюдаю лежа на одеяле
как медленно раздвигает пространство твоя перламутровая
    спина
и как медленно ты вдыхаешь в себя теплый суховатый воздух

я ебусь где угодно – в бутонах цветов
в раздевалках детских балетных школ
ничего меня не остановит
и я буду ебстись так как считаю нужным и столько сколько
    считаю нужным
я пидараска я лесбуха паршивая
и даже если вы убьете меня я буду ебаться в ваших мечтах и
    кошмарах
да я лесбиянка и нет у меня органов других
и живот мой испещерен натруженными сосками
и ноги мои как расписные покрыты влажными вульвами
я в ваших мечтах и кошмарах превратилась в коварную плоть
это взрыв нет это крики гиены
смрадная пасть гиены дрожит от вожделенья над нежными
    розовыми головами младенчиков голубоглазых
их роднички еще не затянулись но гиена розовую кожу
    осквернила
это взрыв и сотни рук потянулись к детским телам под
    гиеновый визг

утопия – розовый лепесток нежная как внутренняя сторона
    бедра любимого тела
утопия мертвая точка и хохот старого пидора

мне кажется пахнет пургой и еще немного хлебом
    обожженным
нет не хлебом но тяжелым натруженным телом городской
    маяты
черным черно пишут черные сапоги по мокрой брусчатке
черным черно в разрыве мы пребываем

it is the victory of a calm stomach
I watch lying on a blanket
how your mother-of-pearl back slowly spreads open the space
and how you slowly inhale warm, barely dry air.

I fuck anywhere—in flower blossoms
in the changing rooms of children's ballet schools
nothing will stop me
and I will fuck any way I want and as much as I feel is necessary
I am a faggot a lousy lesbo
and even if you kill me, I will continue fucking in your dreams and
    nightmares
yes, I am a lesbian, and I have no other organs
and my stomach is littered with tense nipples
and my legs are covered with wet vulvas in a pattern
in your dreams and nightmares, I have turned into predatory flesh
it's an explosion, no, these are the hyena's howls
the hyena's stinky mouth quivers from desire above the tender pink
    heads
of blue-eyed babies
their fontanels are still not healed, but the hyena has already
    desecrated the pink skin
it's an explosion, and hundreds of hands are stretched toward
    children's bodies
accompanied by the hyena's howls.

utopia—a pink petal tender like the inner side of the beloved's
    thigh
utopia is a dead end and an old pederast laughing

it seems that it smells like a snowstorm and a little bit like burned
    bread
no, not bread, but the heavy tired body of city unrest
black-on-black is the writing of black boots on wet cobblestones
and we find ourselves in black-on-black torn space

эй ты!
и распахивается над землей флуоресцирующий небесный
    пейзаж
кто там лежит в складочках тьмы немытой
эй ты!
чьи руки тяжелые скрещены на груди
и тепло такое мягкое как лапка утопии исчезает в черной
    прорези земляной
пахнет пургой
пахнет уставшим телом и не видно в слепоте близкого сердца
оно немое разбитое отдает тепло в расцвеченный холодными
    прожекторами воздух
эй ты!
утопия обвилась вокруг шеи ласковым шарфиком застыла

если меня уже нет если я это груда органов бьющихся органов
    теплых
то где мой рот он изранен
рот изранен
эй ты!
черным черно черным по черному распускается дымок
    хранилища слепоты
а над дымком ласковые небеса размежаются по кусочкам по
    полосочкам раздвигаются и над ними
черная пасть истории клацает
эй ты!

мне не страшно
и веки мои тяжелы
мне не страшно
это взрыв
это разрыв
мне не страшно

если ты здесь – отзовись между нами дрожит тяжелый ветер
    он тянется сомнением и опасеньем

hey you!
and above the earth opens up a fluorescent landscape
who is lying there among the folds of dirty darkness?
hey you!
Whose heavy arms are crossed on their breasts
and warmth so soft like utopia's paw disappears in the black
cup of open earth
it smells like a snowstorm
smells like a tired body and it's not visible in the blindness of a
    heart, close to you
it's mute broken down, it gives out warmth in the air, colored by
    cold searchlights
hey you!
utopia embraced your neck like a tender scarf and froze

if I am no longer here if I am a pile of organs pulsing warm organs
the place where my mouth is cut all over
mouth cut all over
hey you!
black-on-black spreads smoke over the stored blindness
and over the smoke tender skies are dividing piece by piece into
    strips
and over them the black mouth of history clacks
hey you!

I am not scared
and my eyelids are heavy
I am not scared
it's an explosion
it's a tear
I am not scared

If you are here—respond between us a heavy wind trembles it lasts
    like a doubt and
apprehension
I don't know what wind is composed of

я не знаю композиции ветра
но я помню необходимый напор мне не страшно
все немного устали
и над нами дымится рассвет бесконечный лучезарный рассвет
и слепые поют в темноте
и комья земли катят между каменных обломанных тел

а снежок такой тихий вьется попадается на язык
и я чувствую нежный холод
и теплую близость мира
и пахнет вьюгой белой

but I remember the necessary force and I am not scared
everyone is a little tired
and above us is a smoky sunrise an endless radiant sunrise
and the blind ones are singing in the dark
and lumps of earth are rolling down among stony
    broken bodies

and snow so quiet it whips around some gets on your tongue
and I feel the tender cold
and warm closeness of the world
and it smells like a white snowstorm

Anna Halberstadt on Translating
Oksana Vasyakina's Poetry

On Collaboration

Oksana told me from the start that her knowledge of English
is quite limited, and therefore she could not be too helpful in
discussing translation.

Our collaboration was quite smooth, comparable to my
experience with many other authors I've translated. I've found that
poets whose writing I admire—like Eileen Myles, Edward Hirsch,
Vladimir Gandelsman, Kestutis Navakas—are real collaborators.
They are open to suggestions, ready to clarify obscure meanings, and
flexible. They are very well read and are ready to accept a suggestion
for an idiom in another language to replace the one in the poem,
etc. It seems that the poets' caliber correlates with their openness
and flexibility. Of course, there are exceptions to every rule.

On the Challenge of Context

"Opera-Ballet Homophobia" is a very passionate poem, full of
resentment, anger against the oppression of LGBT community in
Russia, but also full of love. Oksana uses the word "black" quite a
bit in it. Here are the first three lines of the poem:

> utopia—a dead-end black dot on a collar of an unkempt shirt
> here black-on-black is the writing of a military uniform in the hall of a
>   magnetic metro
> here black-on-black is the writing of a cloudy blind sunrise

Our conversation took place as Black Lives Matter protests in New York were happening right in front of my windows in the Village. We talked about the new meaning of the word "black" in this context. It seems to be replacing "African American" as the politically and morally correct word to identify Americans of African descent. So we discussed how to translate the lines,

> утопия – нежный лепесток на жирных рельсах метро в рывках
>   воздуха бьется
> черным черно пишут каучуковые подошвы черных людей

where the word "black" describes people—but in this context, people in black military uniforms.

Thus instead of translating the second line as "black-on-black is the writing of the vulcanized rubber soles of black people," I chose to translate it this way:

> utopia—a tender petal on greasy metro rails pulses in gusts of air
> black-on-black is the writing of the vulcanized rubber soles of people in
>   black

Oksana and I also discussed lesbian argot in contemporary Russia. Luckily, I just translated a book of poems by Eileen Myles, titled *Selected, Selected*, into Russian a few years ago. And during that process, I corresponded with Masha Gessen about the best way to translate a poem, a kind of hymn to lesbian love, where the word "cunt" is repeated over and over in different contexts. However, to translate words used as slurs to tease and torment LGBT kids in Russian schools was a challenge—one that, hopefully, the translation of this powerful poem overcame.

Poems by Ivan Sokolov

TRANSLATED BY ELINA ALTER

IVAN SOKOLOV is a poet, translator, scholar, and critic from Saint Petersburg, now based in Berkeley, California. He is the author of four books of poetry, and his work has been translated into several languages, including English, German, Greek, Spanish, and Italian. Sokolov was a finalist for the Arkady Dragomoshchenko Award (2016) and has been a resident at Villa Sarkia in Finland (2015), at the Baltic Center for Writers and Translators in Sweden (2019), and at the Writers' House in Peredelkino, Russia (2021). He has participated in the Russo-German poetry project *VERSschmuggel* (2015) and is a member of the editorial board at *GRYOZA*, where he curated an international festschrift for the centenary of Paul Celan.

ELINA ALTER is a writer and translator. Her translations of Alla Gorbunova's short story collection *It's the End of the World, My Love* (Deep Vellum) and Oksana Vasyakina's novel *Wound* (Catapult) are forthcoming. She is the coeditor of *Circumference*, a magazine of translation and international culture.

резцы , держать , середину , шарниры и аляповатых , смэки из душа , из не толще нашего досок

сколоченных ящиков проседать на виду пассажира — мусорогоры ? остатки ? невместившее в сумерках

абрикосов (А как аспирантов как жадной аварии) ? рад что написал , теплое враг прекрасного , пыль ,

в ночи под затменной луной как собачьи хвосты огневеющие патлы пыли , делай как мыльные — не

пропаганда , и то что написано , было , на пблосах веселящего почерка-отправителя , на новый год

хочу подарить тебе свое любимое растение — когда же это закончится обыкновенная , воском и вереском

придавленных постулатов о том , как за углом к гопнику приставать за свободой , мы ли не

праздновали учет собраний митингов зверского счастья , подозреваю что кто-то вынул дно из-под этой

мишени , тело падать и тело виртуальные соревнования по гребле — что и выбрать , написанное скоплено

в диапазоне подожди не новостная ли это струится в покальываниях , я покажу тебе всякого вижена гон

одноты , надо только перестать по клавишам и дело в пальцах , склада фанерных структур — то как я и

я определяем операцию точечной вылазки из авангарда любви , биографический перешеек , лес бы ты

отсюда пока в нас обоих не влепили по повестке в лирком , синие красивые фиолетовые каждые две

недели новые волосы как у меня подхватившей волны , я пока жду тебе всякого выжена дробь либо

ты и в рестрикте́д эрино пронеся мои снопья акации , снопья чего , акация , это такое приложение для

заплетания ног , эта строка растет себе вправо и никаким препаратом , ветр , снимать , годовая облако

противоречий , деньги снимают с нас отпечатки падения , делать падать , делать исчезать , делать

подставленных кластеров возмущение , лестница пазвука и вторая , чудовищная лестница коротнувшихся

трансформаторов , то что подходит к концу зачинаясь с еще более веским присловьем , мягкое тело года ,

его сосуды , его кипеть на огне подземельном , его бесчисленные города где другие уповают плашмя ,

его кроме довящаяся душевая , видеть вспышки на темени взгорья , ластиться к не вчера промертвым

письменам , доверий припорошенная палатка или колесо ожидания , что же ты , дело , делаешь со мной ,

incisors , hold it , the median , chintzy and hinges , pics from shower , not thicker than ours planks pallets are hammered out of sagging in view of the passenger — trashmounds ? remainders ? unaccommodated in the dusk of apricots (A as in aspirants as in ravening accident) ? glad you wrote , warmth the enemy of beauty , dust , at night under the endarkened moon like dogs' tails blazening dreadlocks of dust , when in rheums — do like the residents , that which was written , taking place , over the lines of a nitrous script-conveyer , for new year's i wanted to give you my favorite plant when will it end regularis , wax and wildflower squashed postulates about how , to put the gopnik up against the wall for his freedom , didn't we celebrate the tally of gathering rallies of bestial happiness , i suspect someone took the bottom out from under this target , down-body and body-virtual crewing competition — just pick one , that which is written collects in that interval wait-isn't-that-the-feed-surging-in-tingles , i'll show you a vision hustling aloneliness , you just need to stop it with the keys and it's a feat of pliance , warehouse of plywood structures — that is i and i plotting the mission of sting operations from the vanguard of love , biographical isthmus , wood you out of here before we both get nailed with a subpoena to the lyrkom , blue beautiful violet every two weeks new hair like the wave sweeping me up , i'll shew you divisions rustling solubles or you carrying my bursts of acacias even into the hieleras , bursts of what , acacia , it's like an app for tailing your tongue , this line just keeps growing right and no prescription will , winde , set off , annually contradictions cloud , the money offsets our impressions of falling , doing falls , doing disappears , doing indignation of positioned clusters , ladder of adventitious sound , and the second , monstrous ladder of burn-out circuits , that which approaching the end begets with an even weightier adage , soft body of the year , its vessels , its to boil over a subterrestrial flame , its countless cities where others abjectly dream , its otherwise stiflingly shower stalls , to see flashing climb the gloaming mountainrise , cleaving to well-dead glyphs , powder-swept tent of confidences or the waiting wheel , what are you , the deed , doing to me , to all of them , how to action this actuality , reader , lungs are for breathing , and he ,

со всеми ними , как действовать эту действительность , читатель , используй легкие чтобы дышать , и тот , кто начертил тушью следы животных без формы и языка на полу бартовского вагона , на новом канале « выпученные носы » серия постов о беженцах из логики счастья , мама , как же я им , связанный по листам и экранам и абрисам , ртами изображая А : америка — или в переводе на общеязычный , aspergō , на площади ишемического единения , в катапультах видоискателей зеленые нити , прорезать , глаза корпусу выступающих за надежду и второй оборот дления , милый мир , как же мы тебя вчера нехватали , что бы сказал президент шредер , и женщина с глазами-павианами , допытывающаяся у каждого , как падает пыль , почему , она начинает падать , где слом , там и объем , где теперь ваши звуковысоты , мыслей игольчащаяся , игольчащаяся , видеть сполохи по всему его телу , в этой пуле еще хватит отверстий , и с того дня мы дальше не читали

who sketched in india ink the traces of animals w/out form and language on the floor of the bart car , on the new *noses blaring* channel a series of posts about refugees from the logic of happiness , mom , what about them how do i , being tied up page and screen and alineation , mouths doing an A : america — or in the common tongue , aspergō , on ischemic unity square , in viewfinder catapults the green filaments , cutting through , eyes of the corps uprising for hope and for the coming of another round of perpetuity , dear world , how you were dismissed yesterday , what would president schreder say , and the woman w/ baboons for eyes , interrogating everyone as to , how dust falls , and why , does it begin to fall , where there's a split , there's a span , where now are your pitchspaces , thoughts aneedle with , thought beneedlinging , to see sparks along his entire body , still enough holes in this bullet , since that day we read no longer

O R T

прекрасен как

рисунок   ты   прекрасен   ты

революция грезы

ненадёжен

парящие   идут , кстати , подороже прочих , хотя и у них

в замешательстве власти   желания в дрожи   не ознакомился с бюллетенем распада

и этих искр ,   расплещущих , как хочу и тебя

но не слабее же в самом деле

и этот , пленительный , как краски и крики ,   как когда помню

он проходит   и он

и тем , что   так   или   так   за поворотом поджигающим поворот   нагибается — и лицо

уцелевшая вспышка

стремительнее этих слов обращаются подсвеченные силуэты   там , где остров захвачен красками , криками   почему ты так смотришь

как и тогда   да , как и сейчас   снимком за снимком   внимания   у меня , помнишь ,   ещё был такой

закрутились ,   и вёртят ,

→ рот пожирает рот   этих взломали ещё при прошлом   но , если и познал , то исключительно по касательной   но ребёнок

так может и разорваться по новой   замедленное письмо паллиативных конечностей по кривой друг от друга   веско или нет , но , описав ,

может , восемнадцатый , опять в тот же луч глазами вперёд   но ведь не взлетели же , понимаешь   катятся , и беззвучная

музыка чужой речи   ты ещё тогда мне сказал   слишком тупые лезвия , упадёшь   в подворотне   и отвернулся   ударить хвостом

к встрече с торцом виража   когда вложил кисть тебе   сопротивление невозможности   эхолокацией сбитой со крылатых эта ещё есть то , грудину в прямо а кто там признавался   в грудь   эти волосы , я серьезно , лучшее , что   воспламенился без кислорода   в любви на катке и кому ?

наклоняется — и неопознанный пар изо рта , или точнее   а если не развороты ? невесомое равенство ? варианты влюбленных   поэт похожее бы написал : высоко

над балконами   из стен   вылезают каменные пары мужчин   и слабый рожок , блядь , сообщает   за подписью : ПАСТЬ ДИСТАНЦИЯ

волоча ноги к торгам на рынке утрат   в кольце гамящих голосов   как по писаному рассекаем   полными пригоршнями

барахтаешься в ледяной ряби , в барабане человеческого стекла   ответ , прокол легкого   и вся переписка наружу

И ЧЕРТЯТ
ПО ЛЬДУ

а кто вам так проявлял ?   если бы мог , сказал , написал первыми буквами : *я не боюсь хотеть тебе принадлежать*   поражает — Эрот

никогда задержаться , как встарь   стояли снаружи почти за руку   а они круг за кругом   остальное — не глубже прожектора

тебя , тебя тоже   и тебя , но не *так* , а *так*   в одном направлении счастья , свободно не задевая за перегородку

клик за кликом   только речь не   разевав скоротечные рты , смех   отстраняешься , а   как же иначе

о птицах   лирическую адресацию начинили эквивалентом   несется навстречу стреноженным огням

массового уничтожения   а я-то думал , только у *желания* есть такой суффикс   и всего-то

на четыре прихотливо ускользающих вдоха меня старше , отчего только заводит   когда раз за разом

упоенно , что ты прекрасен   удар   *так прекрасен*

на расстоянии вытянутой —   подражает —   строки

O R T

dream revolution   you're   beautiful as

beautiful   you're

the sketch unreliable

the soaring   going for more than the others , actually , though they too

muddled shivering by force by desire

failed to read through the devastation newsletter

but really not weaker than   and these sparks ,   spillingly the way i want you , and

he passes   and he does   and this one , enthralling like the colors and cries   like when i remember

and that , which   like that   or   like that   taking a turn setting a turn alight   inclines—and his face   the surviving flare

fleeter than these words fly the lit silhouettes   there , where the island is conquered by colors , cries   why are you looking at me like that

just like before   yes , like now   shot after shot   of attention   remember , once i had   another one like this

spinning   and whirling   so the child

mouth devouring mouth   those got hacked way back during   but even if i did know him , it was tangential

can implode again in a different   the slowed-down writing of palliative limbs coasting away from each other   so it sank in , or not , describing

maybe the eighteenth , eyes forward into the same beam   but we didn't combust , you see   rolling along , and the silent

music of other speech   you know the time you pressed my   at epicenter of orbit grows   blades too dull , you'll fall   in the archway   and turned away   a slap of the tail

to a meeting w/ the arc's end   when my wrist entered into your   resistance of the impossible   echolocation w/ down brought wingeds for a trap it's meaning , breastbone right in and who was it anyway confessing   in the chest   that hair , seriously , it's the best that   incinerate without oxygen   their love at the rink and to whom ?

bows , then—unidentified steam from his mouth , or to be more exact   if not turns then ? weightless parity ? lovers variations   a more southerly poet would write , aloft

above the balconies   from within the walls   climb stone couples of men   and a weak-ass horn sings   signature appended : GNASH DISTANCE

dragging your feet to haggle at the loss market   in the ring of roaring voices   skating as scripted   whole fistfuls

floundering in icy ripples , in a vat of human glass   an answer , a lung puncture   *on ice*   and the whole exchange exposed

and who would develop it like this ?   if i could , would say , write just the initial letters : *i am not afraid of wanting to be yours*   *and sketching*   dazzling : Eros

never to be late , like the olden days   delayingly outside almost hand in   while they trace circle after circle   rest is no deeper than a lightbeam

you , and also you , and you too , but not like *that* , like *this*   in the same direction of happiness , freely not brushing the partition

click after click   only it's not about   gawping their fleeting mouths , laughter   pulls away , of course   what else

the birds   the lyric address loaded with its equivalent   traveling toward the hobbl'd lights

of mass destruction   oh see i had thought only *desire* had that prefix   and only

four impulsively evasive breaths older than me , which drives me   as turn after turn

ecstatic , that you are beautiful   a blow   *so beautiful*

within arm's —   doubling   —   speech

O   R   T

Elina Alter on Translating Ivan Sokolov

In an essay for *GRYOZA* (daydream, mirage), an online poetry project for which he is an editor, Ivan Sokolov writes about his poetic fragments as instantiations, collisions and collusions of speech that may be better represented by a multichannel audio installation than by a single voice.

What, then, should translations of these poems be like?

The two fragments here were translated on the occasion of PEN's workshop. In each, several things are always happening at once. There are resonances between words and phrases within a line, across lines, and with other poems in this series; echoes of other languages, including English; convolutions; exploded collocations. The reader is a participant who must wend a way into and through the text. The translator, who is also a reader, winds her way into the text and tries to stay there, to take in the vibe, so to speak.

When I translate poetry, I'm usually trying to convey the semantics of a word. The words of the translated poem should mean roughly the same thing as the words of the original, although they can't and won't, since each language has its own unique series of phonetic, semantic, historical associations for each word. (I'm paraphrasing Nabokov's lament in "The Art of Translation.")

But in the first of these fragments, Ivan invited me to translate the gesture of a phrase: not its literal meaning but the attempt it makes at meaning, and the implication of its use. So a phrase containing a misheard Russian saying, "делай как мыльные – не пропаганда," becomes the similarly skewed "when in rheums—do like the residents."

In the original, kindly Russian saying—"делай, как мы – не пропадешь," meaning "do as we do, and you'll be fine"—Ivan hears a well-intentioned and obscurely dictatorial instruction, containing an implicit threat (what happens if you *don't* do as we do?). The mishearing, a key element in Ivan's work, depends on the way these words sound in Russian. Thanks to sonic similarities, the proverb transforms into "do like the soaps/the soapy ones, that's not propaganda," effecting in the reader a jab of recognition, confusion, clarity, appreciation, amusement. The autocratic aspect is brought to the surface as the proverb tries to preemptively defend itself. And there's the slightly absurdist and surprisingly tactile introduction of the soap.

In the translation, the likewise well-meaning "when in Rome, do as the Romans do" becomes the slightly slimy "when in rheums," borrowing some of the original's weird new slippery quality. And "do like the residents" echoes, I hope, the original's pedantic (authoritarian?) exhortation not to break with tradition, to blend in.

The Russian saying has long been in use and is quite flexible— you can also do as he does, as I do, and so on. In the postwar period, it was also part of the translated title of an East German TV show meant to get children to exercise (*Mach mit, Mach's nach, Mach's besser*). The English "when in Rome," on the other hand, is itself a translation from Latin of a paraphrase of Saint Augustine by an eighteenth-century pope (and Augustine, too, was originally paraphrasing somebody's well-intended advice). So this translation is just the latest in a series of borrowings and adjustments, maybe a happy coincidence, good static. As in the original poem, the twist of the phrase should set off a little explosion, which should in turn set off another, freeing some energy in the text and in the language.

Still, implosions are also possible. The shape of the second fragment, which was published as *GRYOZA*'s inaugural work, implies, among other things, the revolutions of ice skaters around a rink. The fragment suggests that such eternal and occasionally infernal revolutions are driven by desire. There's a little directional arrow indicating a possible entry point into the fragment, but the routes through it, a labyrinth, are self-evidently various. A reader of the translation eventually winds up at "skating as scripted," which somewhat narrows the width of the original passageway.

This is because the original Russian phrase, "как по писаному рассекаем," is much richer. The conjugation of the verb рассекаем implies the plural first person, sweeps us up—it is we who are slicing, as skaters do, the ice (though in the context of Ivan's other work, it's also possible to read this word as an adjective—someone or something is *sliceable*!). The English phrase, lacking a subject, is less immediate. And the verb itself, "rassekayem," *sounds* like a blade, while the consonant cluster at the start of "scripted" sounds more . . . scratchy.

Another issue is the set phrase "как по писаному," meaning something like "smoothly as though reciting from a written text." Also, because the Russian *to write* and *to pee* are spelled though not pronounced the same way—with one exception, which is the case used here!—there's the slightly gleeful implication of peeing in the snow, which is absent from "scripted," just a reference to a rehearsed and predetermined speech act. The skaters of Ivan's poem seem to have the knowledge of what to do inherent in them, which is what desire feels like; the translated skaters require a script.

Desire moves the poet, too, while the translator works from a script, trying to understand and act out the original impulse. Happily, translation as a field of activity *is* a multichannel installation, in the sense that multiple translators of the same text will produce the polyphony already present in each of these fragments. And a reader making a way through will, I hope, feel compelled to call out something neither the translator nor the author would have dreamed of.

Poems by Ekaterina Simonova

TRANSLATED BY KEVIN M. F. PLATT

EKATERINA SIMONOVA was born in 1977 in Nizhny Tagil. She graduated from the philology department at the Nizhny Tagil State Social Pedagogical Academy. She is the author of six books, including *Byt' malchikom* (*To Be a Boy*, 2004), *Sad so ldom* (*Garden with Ice*, 2011), *Gerbariy* (*Herbarium*, 2011), *Vremya* (*Time*, 2012), *Yelena. Yabloko i ruka* (*Yelena. Apple and Hand*, 2015), and *Dva yeyo edinstvennikh platya* (*Two of Her Only Dresses*, 2020). Her poetry has been translated into English, Slovenian, and Ukrainian. In 2020, she was shortlisted for the Andrei Bely Prize and won the journal *Novyi mir*'s Anthology Prize. She is the curator of a series of Ekaterinburg-based poetry readings called "Poetry About . . . ," the curator of the poetry series *In Versia*, and the coordinator of the all-Russian literary-critical prize Neistoviy Vissarion (Unhinged Vissarion). She lives in Ekaterinburg and works at the Sverdlovsk Oblast V.G. Belinsky Universal Scientific Library.

KEVIN M. F. PLATT is a professor of Russian and East European studies at the University of Pennsylvania, where he directs the periodic Russian-American poetry translation symposium "Your Language, My Ear." His scholarly work focuses on Russian poetry, culture, and history. His translations of Russian poetry have appeared in journals such as *World Literature Today*, *Jacket2*, *n+1*, and *Fence*. He is the author or editor of several scholarly books, the most recent of which is *Global Russian Cultures* (University of Wisconsin Press). He was editor and lead translator for *Hit Parade* (Ugly Duckling Presse), a collection of contemporary poetry by the Latvia-based group Orbita.

Рядом с ее телом, на прикроватной тумбочке,
Нашли записку на испанском:
«Они не успели догнать меня на своих крыльях».
Фраза была написана красным карандашом,
Его потом нашли в кармане халата, вместе с помадой.
Грифель был сильно скошен, как и помада –
Ее следы еще оставались в углах вялых старческих губ.

Дети, внуки, правнуки стояли вокруг.
Говорить было не о чем. Этого ждали уже давно.
Была поздняя осень. Рябиновые грозди за окном,
Падающие ягоды, выклеванные, раздавленные,
Кажущиеся на асфальте следами помады, крови,
Гвоздичными измочаленными лепестками.

Через девять дней пошел снег.
Не знаю, зачем я сейчас об этом пишу.
Я выходила на улицу - вдох-выдох –
Выдыхала воздух, точно стеклянный сосуд,
Он лопался, как будто был с тайным изъяном,
Внутри него оказывались осколки сухих листьев, запах табака,
Какой-то мутный – болотный, нефритовый – свет.

На сороковой день я подошла к ее дому, подняла голову –
В окне кухни отражались тени –
То ли ветви рябины, то ли какие-то крылья.
С ночи был сильный ветер. Стекло вдруг хрустнуло,
Жалобно зазвенело, посыпалось вниз.
В тот день впервые за долгое время
Я смогла дышать, не чувствуя боли в груди и висках.

От нее у меня осталось то, что нельзя никому передать –
Не могу, не хочу, не буду –
Ее нос, ее подбородок, медленный низкий голос, любовь

Next to her body, on the night table
They found a note in Spanish:
"They couldn't catch me with their wings."
The phrase was written with a red pencil
That they later found in the pocket of her bathrobe, along with her
    lipstick.
The pencil lead was worn unevenly, just like the lipstick—
Its traces still remained at the corners of her sagging, aged lips.

Children, grandkids, and great-grandkids stood around her.
There was nothing to talk about. This was long expected.
It was late fall. Rowan clusters outside the window:
Falling berries, pecked at, trampled flat
On the asphalt, looking like streaks of lipstick, or blood
Like tattered carnation petals.

Nine days later it snowed.
I don't know why I'm writing about this now.
I went outside—inhale, exhale—
Exhaled the air like it was a glass vessel;
It burst, as though it had a hidden flaw,
Inside it were shards of dry leaves, the smell of tobacco,
Some kind of murky—swampy, jade—light.

On the fortieth day I went over to her house, looked up.
Shadows reflected in the kitchen window,
Maybe rowan branches, maybe some kind of wings.
There'd been strong winds since the night. Suddenly the glass
    cracked
With a plaintive ringing and showered down.
That day for the first time in a long while
I could breathe without feeling pain in my chest and temples.

What I have left of her I can't pass on to anyone—
Can't, won't, don't want to—
Her nose, chin, her measured, low voice, love

К вещам, о которых не следует говорить,
Ее предсмертная записка, которую я ношу в кармане пальто.
Каждый раз, засовывая туда руку, касаюсь слов
«Они», «крылья», «догнать» и каждый раз

Понимаю, что они все ближе и ближе.

For things one shouldn't talk about,
Her deathbed note, which I carry in my coat pocket.
Every time I put my hand in I touch the words
"They," "wings," "catch" and every time

I know they're getting closer and closer.[1]

---

1 Translated by Irina Barclay, Kit Eginton, Victoria Juharyan, Martha Kelly, Ainsley Morse, Kevin M. F. Platt, and Michael Wachtel at the Translation Workshop of the American Association of Teachers of Slavic and East European Languages.

В секонде вышла на новый уровень пользователя:
научилась подбирать вещи на Елену Федоровну
без Елены Федоровны.
Секрет прост – просто нужно надеть рубашку на себя:
если мне тесновата, то ей как раз в самый раз.

Так были куплены, к примеру,
розовая футболка с бледным геометрическим принтом,
напечатанным с изнаночной стороны,
и португальский пиджак из искусственной овчинки,
выкрашенной в синий цвет.
Хоть на поминки, хоть в театр.

Поэтому пошли в театр.
Представление давали швейцарцы –
из испанской жизни
с французским акцентом.

Молодые актеры играли старых актеров,
старые актеры играли тоже старых актеров,
все вместе играли то ли Тристана и Изольду,
то ли Сальвадора и Гала,
были обещаны и представлены акробатические и иные этюды,
барабанная дробь, бесшабашная буффонада,
деревянные куклы, задыхающийся скафандр,
сольное и хоровое пение.

«Смотри, – сказал в антракте зритель позади меня, –
они же все в морских пляжных полосатых костюмах,
настоящее ретро,
я прямо так и вижу пустынный Кадакес,
сухую траву, море до горизонта, свежая рыба на ужин,
любовь, воздух,
как много воздуха!»

They gave me the next customer level at the secondhand store:
I learned how to pick out things for Elena Fedorovna,
In Elena Fedorovna's absence.
The secret is simple—you just have to put on a shirt yourself:
If it's a little tight on me, then it's just right for her.

That's how I bought, for example,
A pink T-shirt with a pale geometric design,
printed inside out,
and a Portuguese artificial shearling jacket,
dyed midnight blue.
Wear it to a funeral, or wear it to the theater.

So we went to the theater.
It was a Swiss production
on life in Spain
with a French accent.

Young actors played old actors,
old actors also played old actors,
and together they were playing either Tristan and Isolde
or Salvador and Gala;
they promised and delivered acrobatic and other etudes,
drum rolls, a wanton buffonade,
wooden dolls, a suffocating spacesuit,
solo and choral song.

"Look," said a spectator behind me during intermission,
"they're all in striped seaside bathing suits,
real retro;
it's just how I imagine a deserted Cadaqués:
dry grass, sea right up to the horizon, fresh fish for dinner,
love, air,
so much air!"

«Смотри, – сказал зритель впереди меня, –
ведь эти костюмы – точно отсылка к тюремным робам:
их слишком много, есть только сожаления о прошлом,
они никому не нужны, они в клетке,
ничего больше не будет, только одиночество
среди таких же, как ты».

«Правда – подумала я, –
это всего лишь то, что ты называешь правдой».

"Look," said a spectator in front of me,
"those costumes directly reference prison uniforms:
there are too many of them and only regret for the past;
no one needs them; they're in a cage;
there's no future, only solitude
among others just like you."

"True," I thought,
"It's just what you call the truth."

Сволочью был М.А. Булгаков:

Бросил одну жену, затем другую, третью увел из семьи.

Сволочью был Н.А. Заболоцкий:

Тиранил кроткую жену, на новые простыни выдавал деньги,

Отсчитывая мелочь до копейки, укажет, какого цвета купить,
сколько штук.

Сволочью был А.А. Блок:

Просто не хотел заниматься с женой сексом, потому что
любовь выше этого.

Сволочью был Д.И. Хармс:

Изменял с каждой первой –

Жена, приходя домой, прежде, чем зайти в комнату, стучала
в дверь.

Сволочью был И.А. Бунин:

Привел любовницу в дом, сказал жене: «Моя ученица, будет
жить с нами».

Несчастным человеком был М.А. Булгаков, трагической – его
жизнь:

Был гоним властями, умирал тяжело и долго, не отпускал от себя

Елену Сергеевну, держал ее за руку, но помогал только
морфий.

Несчастным человеком был Н.А. Заболоцкий, трагической –
его жизнь:

Был репрессирован, отсидел восемь лет, стал бояться

Писать так, как стоило, жена ушла к другому, вернулась, но
было поздно.

Несчастным человеком был А.А. Блок, трагической – его
жизнь:

Мучали его сомнения, бессонницы и кошмары,

Тяжелая семейная жизнь, рухнувший привычный мир.

Несчастным человеком был Д.И. Хармс, трагической – его
жизнь:

Был арестован раз, потом второй,

Умер от голода во время блокады в отделении психиатрии
тюремной больницы.

Mikhail Afanasievich Bulgakov was an asshole:
He left one wife, then another; broke up a family to get a third
Nikolai Alekseevich Zabolotsky was an asshole:
He lorded it over his timid wife when he gave her money for new
    sheets,
He would count the pennies and specify colors and quantities to buy.
Aleksandr Aleksandrovich Blok was an asshole:
He just refused to have sex with his wife because love is higher
    than that
Daniil Ivanovich Kharms was an asshole:
Cheated on his wife left and right
When she came home, she used to knock on the door before going in.
Ivan Alekseevich Bunin was an asshole:
He brought his mistress home with him and told his wife: "This is
    my student. She's going to live with us."

Mikhail Afanasievich Bulgakov was an unfortunate man with a
    tragic fate:
Persecuted by the state, he suffered a drawn-out, painful death;
    wouldn't let go of Elena Sergeevna, clung to her hand, but only
    morphine could help.
Nikolai Alekseevich Zabolotsky was an unfortunate man with a
    tragic fate:
Swept up in the Terror, he spent eight years in the camps, and then
    was too scared
To write for real; his wife left him for another, then came back to
    him, but it was too late.
Aleksandr Aleksandrovich Blok was an unfortunate man with a
    tragic fate:
He was tormented by doubts, insomnia, nightmares,
An awful family life, the destruction of the world he knew.
Daniil Ivanovich Kharms was an unfortunate man with a tragic fate:
Got arrested, then arrested again,
He died of hunger during the Leningrad blockade in a prison
    hospital psychiatric ward.

Несчастным человеком был И.А. Бунин, трагической – его жизнь:
Ученица-любовница променяла его на женщину, он сам
Так больше и не вернулся на родину,
В деревню, к бабам, борзым, яблокам, московским колоколам.

Дед одной моей знакомой
В 41-м ушел на фронт, в 42-м попал в плен.
Был отправлен в Бухенвальд. Выжил. В 45-м дружественными
    войсками
Был освобожден, вернулся на родину. Тут же – сослан на Урал
    как враг народа.
Когда вышел, к первой жене не вернулся, бросил за
    ненадобностью.
Остался в Тагиле, пошел в печники.
Взял себе молоденькую – она боялась его называть по имени.
Идти замуж не хотела, но мать заставила, сказала:
«Иначе ты никому не нужным сухоцветом останешься, иначе
    ты мне не дочь».
Работа была хорошая и важная, часто ездил в командировки.
В каждом городе у него было по женщине.
В те годы была острая нехватка в мужском поле.
Женщины знали друг о друге, о семье.

Спрашивали, как у них дела, как дочки учатся,
Как у жены здоровье, передавали им гостинцы,
Благодарили жену за то, что делится необходимым с другими.
Умер в сорок три от пневмонии, когда младшей дочке
    исполнилось пять.
Младшую он, кстати, назвал именем одной из любовниц.
Сказал об этом жене.

Сволочью или несчастным человеком он был?
Мы так и не узнали.
Его жена не рассказала об этом
Ни одной из своих трех дочерей.

Ivan Alekseevich Bunin was an unfortunate man with a tragic fate:
His student-mistress threw him over for a woman, and he could
　　never return to his homeland,
To the countryside, the gals, Borzoi hounds, apples, and the bells
　　of Moscow.

The granddad of one of my girlfriends
Left for the front in '41 and got taken prisoner in '42.
They sent him to Buchenwald. He survived. In '45 the Allied armies
Liberated him and he came back home. They sent him away to the
　　Urals then and there as an enemy of the people.
When he got out he didn't go back to his first wife; had no use for
　　her and abandoned her.
He stayed in Tagil and went to work as a stove setter.
Found a young woman—she was afraid to even say his name.
She didn't want to marry, but her mother forced her, saying:
"Otherwise you'll wind up a useless dried up old flower; otherwise
　　you're no daughter of mine."
He had a good, important job, traveled all the time for work,
A woman in every town.
There was a severe shortage of men in those years.
The women knew about each other, about his family.

They'd ask how are things going at home, how are the girls doing in
　　school?
How's the wife, her health? They'd send little presents,
To thank his wife for sharing an essential need with others.
He died of pneumonia at forty-three, when his youngest daughter
　　was five.
He named the youngest for one of his mistresses, by the way.
Told his wife about that.

Was he an asshole or an unfortunate man?
We never found out.
His wife never told
Any of the three daughters.

Подмышки и ноги бреют легкомысленные женщины.
Так считалось в моем детстве.
Добрые матери, хорошие жены радуют взгляд
Своим золотистым пушком абрикосовым,
Своим темным дымком, похожим
На дымок над огородным костром, когда
Всей семьей, с тещами, детьми, зятьями,
Жгут старую ветошь, кривые палки, ботву,
Пекут картошку в золе, потом едят, обжигаясь,
Пачкая рты и пальцы.

Много было вокруг серьезных, ответственных женщин.

Все они были примером для маленькой девочки —
Будущей доброй матери, хорошей жены.

Летом, когда дома отключали воду,
Бабушка водила меня в городскую баню.
Когда заходили в зал, количество порядочных женщин
Резко увеличивалось. Впрочем, я, как обычный ребенок,
Не размышляла о длине женских интимных волос, зато
Навсегда запомнила пар из разбухшей двери парилки,
Серые тазики, называвшиеся почему-то шайками,
     прилипавшие
К рукам, ступням серые, как тазики, березовые листы.

Взрослые женщины исподтишка разглядывали друг друга,
Смотрели, что им друг в друге не нравится,
К чему можно придраться, кто из них
Самая порядочная женщина, самая хорошая жена.

В девяностые вдруг оказалось,
Что нас воспитывали неправильно.
Женщина должна быть свободной, свободная женщина
Бреет волосы, чтобы ни золотистый пушок абрикосовый,
Ни темный дымок, похожий на дымок на костром,

Women who shave their legs and armpits are frivolous.
That's what we thought when I was young.
Kind mothers and good wives are a joy to see
With their golden apricot fuzz,
Their dark down, that looks like
The haze over a fire in the yard when
The whole family, with mothers and sons-in-law and kids,
Burns old castoffs, crooked sticks, haulm,
Bakes potatoes in the coals, and then eats them, getting singed,
Smearing mouths and fingers.

There were a lot of serious, responsible women around.

They all set an example for a little girl—
A future kind mother and good wife.

In the summer, when they turned off the hot water at home
Grandma would take me to the city baths.
When we went into the hall, the number of decent women
    increased
Significantly. Meanwhile, like any small child, I
Didn't give a thought to the length of women's pubic hair, but
The cloud bursting from the steam bath door has stayed with me
    forever,
And also the gray tubs, called for some reason *shaiki*, the birch
Leaves, gray like the tubs, that stuck to your hands and feet.

Grown-up women would surreptitiously look each other over,
Picking out things they disliked,
What they could raise an eyebrow at, who of them
Was the most decent woman, the best wife.

In the nineties it suddenly turned out
That we had been misguided in our upbringing.
A woman should be free, and a free woman
Shaves, gets rid of the golden apricot fuzz,

Не выдавали в ней склонность во всем
Слушаться мужа, кормить детей кашей,
Быть слишком серьезной. Привыкали к этой мысли долго,
Переучивались со слезами, но что поделать —
В прессе, в женских журналах неправильного не напишут.

Каждой пришлось определиться,
Что брить, что не брить. В магазинах, потом в каждом доме
У каждого члена семьи появился свой отдельный станок для
    бритья —
Независимо от пола и возраста.
Много случилось тайных, позорных ссор между женами и
    мужьями,
Обнаружившими утром свои бритвы с прилипшим мокрым
Не живым абрикосовым, не трепещущим облачно-темным,
А банно-серым жениным подмышковым волоском.

О таком не расскажешь друзьям,
Не поплачешься за парой пива, поднимут на смех.

Что я думала об этом? Не знаю. Мне было все равно.
«Не волосы делают женщину привлекательной», — шептала,
Подбривая ноги перед свиданием, представляя
Женщин нового времени, которые могли бы стать мне
    примером.

Прошло почти двадцать лет.
Все-таки все мы остаемся в душе маленькими,
С каждым годом понимаю я, радуюсь,
Видя, что снова становятся важными
Знакомые с детства вещи:

Как появляется вновь золотистый пушок абрикосовый на ногах,
Темный дымок подмышками, похожий
На дымок над огородным костром, поскольку
Действительно, как мне и говорили, вечны идеалы моего детства:

The dark down, like the haze over a fire.
Not to let on to a tendency to be obedient
To her husband in everything, to feed the children kasha,
To be too serious. It took a while to get used to this idea:
We tearfully unlearned and relearned, but what can you do?
The press, the women's magazines wouldn't print untruths.

Everyone had to make up their mind,
What to shave, what not to shave. In the stores, and then in every
    home,
Shaving equipment appeared for every member of the family—
Regardless of age and gender.
There were a great many secret, disgraceful fights between wives
    and husbands
Who found damp hair in their razors in the morning,
Not the vibrant apricot or shivery dark-smoky kind,
But bath-gray women's armpit hair.

That's something you can't tell your friends,
Can't cry about over a couple of beers; they'd just laugh at you.

What did I think about all this? I don't know. I didn't care.
"It's not hair that makes a woman attractive," I whispered
While shaving my legs to go on dates, imagining
Women of the new era who could set an example for me.

Almost twenty years have passed.
All the same, in our souls we're still children,
As I understand better each year, joyfully
Seeing how the familiar things of childhood
Become important again:

How golden apricot fuzz reappears on legs,
Dark down in armpits, like
The haze over a fire in the yard, because
It's true, just like they told me, the ideals of childhood are eternal:

Порядочные женщины,
Добрые матери,
Хорошие жены.

Decent women,
Kind mothers,
Good wives.

Из цикла «Лето»

Лето. Четверг

На ужин сегодня радужная форель.
Лена уехала на работу забрать форель.
У Лены очень хорошая работа – постоянно что-то оттуда
    приносит:
То колбасу со скидкой, то черешню за 160р/килограмм,
То домашнее масло, теперь вот свежую форель – уже в третий
    раз.

Все ждут форель: бутылка чилийского белого в холодильнике,
Дыня «Колхозница» на десерт – пахнет душно и сладко.
Я лежу на диване, умирая от жары, и жду.
Рядом со мной ждет кот Федор – ему ничего не достанется,
Но он ждет за компанию, исполняя обязанности кота.

Когда приезжает Лена, мы все встречаем ее в коридоре.
В руках у нее пакет. В пакете лежит форель.
Форель приятно тяжелая. Чешуя ее переливается.
Времени на часах уже девять вечера,
Но форели сегодня быть, несмотря ни на что.

Я и коты сидим на кухне, смотрим, как Лена готовит форель:
Надрезает плоть, вкладывает в нее, как пальцы в рану, лимон,
Делает из фольги ладью, готовит луковую подушку,
Просит включить духовку на 180 градусов.

Мы накрываем на стол. Режем огурец – он хорошо идет к
    рыбе.
Достаем охлажденное вино из холодильника.
Жалуясь друг другу «жарко, ужас, с ума сойти, как жарко»,
Открываем духовку, разворачиваем фольгу, сглатываем слюну.

from the cycle "SUMMER"

SUMMER: THURSDAY

Tonight there's rainbow trout for dinner.
Lena went into work to get the trout.
Lena has a great job—she's always bringing something home:
First discount salami, then cherries for 160 rubles a kilo,
Then homestyle butter, and then fresh trout—already for the third
    time.

Everyone is waiting for the trout: a bottle of Chilean white in the
    fridge,
"Collective Farmgirl" melon for dessert—smells fragrant and
    sweet.
I'm lying on the couch, dying of hunger, waiting.
Fedor the cat is waiting next to me. He won't get anything,
But he's keeping me company waiting, performing his cat duties.

When Lena arrives, we greet her in the hallway.
She's carrying a bag. In the bag is the trout.
The trout is pleasantly heavy. Its scales glisten.
It's already nine o'clock,
But tonight there'll be trout, come what may.

The cats and I sit in the kitchen and watch Lena cook the trout:
She pierces the flesh and inserts lemon, like fingers into a wound,
Makes a boat out of foil, makes a bed of onion,
Tells us to turn the oven on to 180.

We set the table. Slice cucumbers—they're great with the fish—
Get the chilled wine from the refrigerator.
Complaining "It's crazy hot, drives you nuts, so hot,"
We open the oven, unfold the foil, salivate and gulp.

Писать о маленьком тихом счастье – бессмысленнее всего.
Нет ничего скучнее стихов о том, что все хорошо.
Успокаивает одно: перед смертью
Я точно буду вспоминать не свои и не чужие стихи,

А вот этот июль, горячий, как только вскипевший чайник,
Розовое мясо форели, почти проглоченную рыбную косточку,
Повлажневший от холода бокал с шардоне,
Тоскливо принюхивающегося кота Тимофея,
Лену, гордую собой и рыбой, повторяющую снова и снова:
«Ну молодец же ведь я, ну скажи, молодец?»

Лето. Суббота

Клевер: сломанный, розовый, мохнатый, цветущий.
На озере: позади березы, сосны, беседки, мангалы,
помятая трава, мятые, не до конца отдохнувшие лица,
трезвые семейные таджики, узбеки
сидят на отдельном пляже от употребляющих русских,
маленькие дети кидают в уток пластиковые стаканы с водой.
Впереди – пустое озеро с маленькой белой лодочкой вдалеке,
В лодочке – двое маленьких и одна большая в панамках.
Плакаты напоминают: «Купаться запрещено».

Справа от нас: крупная, мясистая, с белым трясущимся животом,
с соломенными волосами, фотографирует, кричит знакомым:
«Дочь-то у вас фотомодель, готовая фотомодель,
Смотри как позирует – ничо объяснять не надо»,
Дочь краснеет, отец кивает, мать смеется,
Достает еще пива, чипсы, полотенце, помидоры.

Слева: в полосатом длинном платье, пьет только воду,
Тихо рассказывает: «Когда она рожала, разорвалась так,
Что пришлось накладывать швы. Несколько часов «на живую»
    шили.

It's completely pointless to write about a quiet little pleasure.
Nothing's more of a bore than poems about everything being fine.
The only comfort is this: when I lie dying
It's certain that I'll remember neither my own nor others' poetry,

But this July instead, hot as a boiled teapot,
The trout's pink meat, a fishbone nearly swallowed,
A glass of cold chardonnay sweating with condensation,
Timofey the cat, sorrowfully taking in the smells,
Lena, proud of her fish and herself, repeating over and over:
"Well I'm something aren't I? Say it: I'm something!"

SUMMER: SATURDAY

Clover: broken, pinkish, fluffy, blooming.
At the lake: behind us are birches, pines, pavilions, grills,
The trampled grass, crumpled, not entirely rested faces;
Sober families of Tajiks, Uzbeks
Sit on a separate beach away from the Russian drinkers,
Little kids toss plastic cups full of water at the ducks.
Before us is the empty lake with a little white boat in the distance;
In the boat are two young ones and one woman in sunhats.
Posters instruct: "Bathing prohibited."

To the right: a big meaty woman with a jiggly white belly,
With flax blond hair, takes pictures, yelling at her friends:
"Your daughter is like a model, a born model,
Look how she's posing, doesn't need nothing explained."
The daughter blushes, father nods, mother laughs;
Gets more beer, chips, a towel, tomatoes.

To the left: a woman in a long, striped dress, drinking just water,
Quietly explains: "When she was giving birth, she tore so much
They had to use stitches. They were sewing her up for hours with
    no anesthetic.

Боялась, что зашьют даже то, что не надо.
Три года прошло, болит до сих пор. Но это же ради ребенка,
Так что неважно».

Замолкаем. Жужжит пчела, звонит чей-то сотовый,
В мутной воде плывет мутная стая мальков.
Двенадцатилетняя, бледная, с верблюжьими костлявыми
    коленками
Входит в воду, разгоняет мальков, оборачивается назад,
Развевается на вялом ветру яркий шарф.
Вторая – энергичная, громкая, с рыхлым животом,
Готовится снова снимать, учит:
«Волосы назад откинь, грудь вперед, улыбайся сильнее».
Двенадцатилетняя бормочет «сейчас, сейчас»,
Откидывает волосы назад, улыбается, пытается не щуриться,
Выставить отсутствующую грудь вперед.
Мечтает, как выложит завтра все в инстаграмм.

Лето. Воскресенье

Видели коров, стоящих по колено в реке Утка.
Музей Мамина-Сибиряка был закрыт – все еще карантин.
Зато открыты гора, поля, лес. Пошли на гору,
Дышали горячим воздухом, набрали всего, чего только можно –
Таволги, зверобоя, укусов слепней, фотографий на фоне
    природы.

Видели оленей, выпрашивающих яблоки и капусту,
Свиней в грязи, лошаденка с соломенной гривой,
Видели хаски – один глаз желтый, другой голубой,
Купили на память о том, что здесь видели, ненужную вещь,
Похожую то ли на рыбу, то ли на бабу, то ли на брюшко жука.

Видели дом моей бабушки, отданный, проданный много раз.
Осталось только пустое место, заросли иван-чая, обломок бревна.

She was afraid they would just stitch up everything there.
That was three years ago and it still hurts. But it's for the sake of a
    child. So it doesn't matter."

We fall silent. A bee buzzes; someone's cell phone rings;
A murky school of minnows passes in the murky waters.
The twelve-year-old girl, pale with bony camel knees,
Heads into the water, chasing minnows away, turns back;
A bright scarf flutters in the feeble wind.
The woman—energetic, loud, with the loose belly,
Gets ready to snap more pictures and directs:
"Throw your hair back, chest forward, smile more."
"Wait a minute, wait a minute," the twelve-year-old mutters,
Throws her hair back, smiles, tries not to squint,
Sticks out her nonexistent chest.
Dreams of posting it all on Instagram tomorrow.

SUMMER: SUNDAY

We saw cows up to their knees in Utka River.
The Mamin-Sibiriak Museum was closed—it was still quarantine.
But the mountains, fields, and forests were open. We went to the
    mountains,
Breathed in the hot air and gathered up everything possible:
Meadow wort, horsefly bites, photos in natural settings.

We saw deer begging for apples and cabbage,
Hogs in mud, a horsey with a flaxen mane;
We saw huskies—one eye yellow and one blue;
As a souvenir of all we'd seen we bought a useless thing
Resembling a fish, or maybe an old lady, or maybe a beetle's belly.

We saw my grandma's house, given away, repeatedly resold.
All that was left was an empty place, clumps of pigweed, broken
    bits of logs.

Все умирает, оставшись без тех, кто его бережет - живое и
    неживое.
Кажется, я ничего не почувствовала.
Кажется, теперь я окончательно поняла, что когда-то тоже умру.

Видели реку Межевая Утка, купались.
Говорили о мужьях, женах, детях, о том,
Какой вкусной кажется еда на свежем воздухе, как здесь
    хорошо.
Возвращаясь обратно, молчали – говорить было не о чем.
Все слова остались там, на берегу, среди черных сосновых
    шишек,
Чужого детства, нашего – навсегда, прости меня и забудь –
    невозвращения.

Everything—both the living and the nonliving—dies when those
    who care for it are gone.
Seems like I felt nothing.
It now seems I've fully understood that I too will die.

We saw the Mezhevaia Utka River and went swimming.
Talked about husbands, wives, children, and about
How delicious food seems in the fresh air, about how nice it is here.
On the way back we were silent—there was nothing to talk about.
All the words were left behind, on the shore, among black
    pinecones,
Someone else's childhood, and our own—our final, forgive me and
    forget—nonreturn.

ДЕВОЧКИ
девочкам посвящается

I

Вчера нашла на работе старые кеды бывшей.
И надо бы выкинуть, на кой они нужны.
А не смогла. Убрала в коробку.
Вот что это?

Раньше мы бухали и трахались.
Разговаривали. Было весело.
А потом она решила родить.
Ну хочет так хочет. Взяли сперму у знакомого,
Договорились. Дело нехитрое: набрала в шприц, сама себе
    ввела.
Повезло с первого раза, прикинь?

Нет, я детей не люблю, но знаешь, стала замечать:
Прихожу домой, а он меня узнает.
Лыбится, дурачок, руки тянет.
Ну и я лыблюсь в ответ, как дура.

Когда она родила сына, секс у нас закончился.
Потом она перестала меня целовать.
Потом обнимать.
Я как-то специально считала:
Она три недели не прикасалась ко мне.
А ведь жили вместе.
А Женька мне, как познакомились, сразу фотку прислала с
    голой грудью.
#нутакое.

Вот так все по глупости и закончилось.
Семь лет, представляешь, семь лет.

GIRLS
dedicated to the girls

I

Yesterday I found my ex-girlfriend's old sneakers at work.
And I should've tossed them what the heck good are they.
But couldn't. I put them back in the box.
So what is that?

We used to get wasted and fuck.
We would talk. It was fun.
And then she decided to have a kid.
Well if that's what she wants. We got semen from a guy we knew,
Made a deal. It was a cinch: she loaded it in a syringe and injected
    it herself.
And get this hit the jackpot on the first try.

No, I don't like kids, but you know, I started noticing:
I get home and he recognizes me.
Gets all smiley, little fool, reaches for me.
And I get all smiley in response, like a fool.

When she had the baby, our sex life ended.
Then she stopped kissing me.
And then hugging.
Once I even kept count:
She didn't touch me for three weeks.
That's while living together.
Meanwhile, as soon as we met, Zhenka sent me a picture of her
    bare breasts.
#gofigure

So it all just ended out of stupidity.
Seven years, can you imagine, seven years.

Все, больше никаких баб с детьми:
Полюбишь, привыкнешь,
А он все равно не твой.

А кеды... Мне вот одна тут ляпнула,
Что, мол, чужое не поднялась рука на помойку выбросить.
Какое чужое? В том-то и дело, что не чужое.

Помню, как мы их покупали.
Помню, под что мы их покупали.
Помню, когда она их оставила.
Прошло уже два года. А вот надо же.

2

Пришла она, значит, после выпускного домой и заявила:
«Мама, папа, я – лесбиянка».
И стоит, вся такая гордая и независимая.
А у самой пальцы дрожат. Я ж вижу.
И почему-то именно эти дрожащие пальцы меня так взбесили.
«Курица безмозглая, – говорю – ты че несешь?!
Мы тя на кой воспитывали? ДЛЯ ЭТОГО?!»

Вечером она домой не явилась. Пофиг, думаю,
Не пропадет. Хотя, конечно, дергаюсь. Так бы и прибила дрянь.
Нашла в контакте пару лесбийских паблов, читала.
Не спала до утра. И такая меня вдруг обида взяла
За всю мою просранную жизнь.
Почему они теперь думают, что только им все можно?

Ну и все. Уже третий год встречаюсь со своей.
В сети и познакомились. Помню, как я ее впервые увидела –
Стоит с этой нелепой обвисшей герберой,

Enough. No more chicks with kids.
You love 'em, get used to them,
But all the same they aren't yours.

But the sneakers . . . One of the others explained
That she couldn't, so she said, throw out someone else's trash.
Someone else's? The whole problem was they weren't just someone's.

I remember when we bought them.
I remember what we bought them for.
I remember when she left them there.
Two years have gone by. What the hell!

2

She came home from the graduation ball and announced:
"Mama, Papa: I'm a lesbian."
And just stands there, all proud and independent.
But her fingers are trembling. I can see it.
And for some reason it was those trembling fingers that made me
    furious.
"You brainless hen, I say, what kinda nonsense are you spouting?!
Why'd we even bring you up? FOR THIS?"

That night she didn't show up at home. So what, I think.
She'll turn up. But of course I'm shaken. Should've smacked her,
    that trash.
I found a couple of lesbian instas. Read them through.
Didn't sleep until morning. And suddenly got so pissed off
Over my whole shitty life.
Why is it they think that for them anything goes now?

So be it. Now I've been dating my own girl for three years already.
We met online. I remember when I first saw her:
Standing there with this idiotic drooping Gerber daisy,

В замызганных рокерских ботинках – дождь был,
И это было так . . . дико и правильно одновременно.

Нет, мужу я сразу сказала, что и как.
И как? Да так и живем. Уже ж 22 года замужем.
Куда я без него?

А он что? Да что он. Психовал сначала, потом привык.
Куда он без меня? Говорю ж: 22 года. Не шутка.
Моя к нам даже на дачу приезжает,
По субботам с Юрой вместе шашлыки жарят.

Вот только дочь он так и не простил.
Во всем, говорит, она виновата.

3

Ее Светой звали. Хорошая такая девочка.
Тот редкий случай, когда Светой называют не блондинок.
Из Екатеринбурга, как ты.
Спокойная такая была, никогда не смеялась –
Только улыбалась немножко.
У нее вся спина, помню, была вся в маленьких родинках.

Только я была молодая, адреналину хотелось.
Ну тут и подвернулась Ксюша,
В «Типичной теме» зацепились языками.
Я два года каждый день письма писала –
Ей это настроение повышало.
Слала подарки ей и ее сыну, а она за эти два года
Даже ни разу в скайп не вышла.
Я кидала деньги на ее телефон – тогда только Ксюша звонила.

In muddy rocker boots—it was raining,
And it was like . . . insane and just right at the same time.

No, I told my husband right away what was up.
And so what? Well our life goes on. I've been married for 22 years.
What would I do without him?

And what about him? So what about him! He freaked out at first,
     then got used to it.
What would he do without me? I'm telling you: 22 years. No joke.
My girl even comes out to the dacha,
She and Yuri grill shashlik together on Saturdays.

But our daughter he just couldn't forgive.
Everything is her fault, he says.

3

She was called Sveta. A good sort of girl.
One of those rare cases of a Sveta who isn't a blonde.
From Ekaterinburg, like you.
A really calm one, never laughed—
Just smiled a little.
Her whole back, as I recall, was covered with little moles.

But I was young. I needed adrenaline.
And right then Ksiusha turned up.
We talked each other's ears off in that café, Typical Topics.
For two years I wrote her a letter every day—
It lifted her mood.
I sent presents to her and her son, but for those same two years
She didn't even Skype once with me.
I put money in her phone account—Ksiusha was the only one
     calling then.

Потом она пропала на две недели.
Потом объявилась, сказала, что ее напоила и изнасиловала
    бывшая.
Сказала, что я в этом виновата,
Потому что я – холодная сука.

Потом ее кто-то еще домогался,
Потом у нее кто-то умер. Во всем этом была виновата я.

Еще у нее была деспотичная мать,
Следившая, не с бабами ли опять дочь сношается,
Поэтому встретиться со мной Ксюша отказывалась.

Когда она предложила расстаться, я была счастлива.

За эти два года я и не заметила,
Как Света исчезла из моей жизни.

Знаешь, я однажды Свете стишок написала:
«Хорошая девочка Света в столице Урала живет».
Дальше не помню, помню только, как она заплакала,
Потому что ей кто-то впервые в жизни написал стихи.

Жаль, что я – сволочь.

4

Я тогда думала, что у меня сердце разорвется.
Мне с близнецами всегда не везло:
Всегда на них западаю.

Она тоже, прикинь, близнец.
Я никогда не знала, что ей придет в голову.

Then she vanished for two weeks.
Then reappeared and said that her ex-girlfriend got her drunk and
 raped her.
Said that this was all my fault.
Because I am a cold bitch.

Then someone else was harassing her;
Then someone died on her. And all of this was my fault.

Also she had a tyrannical mother
Who kept a lookout whether her daughter was rutting with girls
 again,
And so Ksiusha refused to go on dates with me.

When she said she wanted to break up I was relieved.

In those two years I hadn't noticed
That Sveta had disappeared from my life.

You know, I wrote a poem for Sveta one time:
"That lovely girl named Sveta, lives in the Ural capital."
I don't remember the rest. I just remember that she cried
Because it was the first time in her life anyone had written her a
 poem.

It's a shame I'm such a jerk.

4

I thought my heart would burst that time.
I never had any luck with twins:
I always fall for them.

She was a twin, too, get it.
I never knew what she would come up with next.

Пыталась забыть ее, как могла:

Переспала с ее бывшей.
Переспала с ее тремя подругами.
Переспала опять с ней.
Потом переспала с ней и ее другом.
Переспала с девушкой ее брата.
Переспала с ее братом.
Она переспала с моим братом.
Переспала с двумя моими бывшими
И моей нынешней.
Я снова переспала с ней.
И так три года.

Она со своей недавно поженилась,
Ну как поженилась: просто друзей позвали,
Сделали свадебный альбом – так, для себя.
Обе в белых платьях.
За съемку заплатили 80 косарей.
Откуда знаю? Да так, случайно увиделись в клубе,
Поболтали, она показала фотки.
Попрощались. Как будто ничего не было.
Я даже не помню ее фамилии.

5

И вот эта байда уже пять лет, представляешь,
Пять лет. Муж уезжает в командировку,
Я приезжаю на неделю к ней.
Какой муж? Ну как какой. Бывший.
Ну не одобряет он. А они работают вместе.
Дети ей вообще сказали:
Будешь с этой видеться – больше не будешь общаться с
    внуком.
Ну а что она могла сделать?

I tried to forget her any way I could:

I slept with her ex.
Slept with three of her girlfriends.
Slept with her again.
Then I slept with her and her boyfriend.
Slept with her brother's girlfriend.
Slept with her brother.
She slept with my brother.
Slept with two of my exes
And with my current girl.
I slept with her again.
And so on for three years.

She and her girlfriend recently got married.
I mean, you know, married: got some friends together
And made a wedding album—like, for themselves.
Both in white dresses.
Paid 80 grand for the photography.
How do I know? We ran into each other in a club.
We got to talking and she showed me the photos.
And we said goodbye. Like there'd never been anything between us.
I don't even remember her last name.

5

So this saga is already five years old, can you believe it?
Five years. Her husband goes away on a business trip.
And I move in with her for a week.
Which husband? You know which. Her ex.
But he doesn't approve. And they work together.
Her kids told her right out:
If you get together with that one, you'll never see your grandson
    again.
So what was she supposed to do?

Вот так и живем пять лет: неделю тайком вместе, потом
Я ухожу от нее на работу, как обычно,
После работы еду к себе домой.
Еще неделю не разговариваем. Иногда просто хочется
    сдохнуть.
Просто хочется сдохнуть.

Ничего не могу поделать с собой.
Каждый раз возвращаюсь к ней, как полная идиотка.

Пыталась встречаться с другими.
Будешь смеяться, но попадаются
Девушки только с ее именем.
У меня теперь целый список: Н1, Н2, Н3.

С каждым разом от меня будто отрывают
По кусочку. Она так всегда от куска хлеба
Отщипывает по крошке, не ест, а просто отщипывает,
Даже не замечая, что делает.
Не знаю, насколько меня еще хватит.

А хочется-то, знаешь, совсем немного:
Сесть уже наконец на жопу в одном месте,
Жарить ей тупые котлеты, вязать ей тупой свитер,
Примеряя тогда, когда нужно примерить, а не раз в два месяца,
Утром и вечером
Трогать одни и те же сиськи. Какжевсезадолбало. Все.

И на море.

6

Девочки, будьте женственными!
Ведь вы должны нравиться!
Я вот за собой всегда слежу

We've been living like that five years: in secret together for a week,
    then
I go off to work, as usual,
And after work go home to my own place.
We don't talk for a week. Sometimes I just want to die.
Just want to die.

I can't do anything with myself.
I go back to her every time, like a total idiot.

I've tried seeing other people.
You'll laugh, but I keep just getting
Girls with her name.
I have a whole list now: N1, N2, N3.

Every time it's like something is being torn out of me
Bit by bit. She always pinches off like that from a piece of bread,
Pinches off a crumb, without eating it, just pinches it off.
Not even noticing what she's doing.
I don't know how much of me is left.

And I don't want much at all, you know:
To sit my ass down at last in one place,
Cook her stupid meatballs, knit her stupid sweater,
Checking if it fits when I need to, and not once every two months,
Touching the same tits,
Morning and night. I'msofuckingoverthis. That's it.

Off to the beach.

6

Girls, be feminine!
You should be attractive!
As a woman, I never let myself go,

И хотела бы, чтобы рядом со мной была такая же –
Ухоженная, настоящая женщина.

Поэтому с феминисткой я бы точно встречаться не стала:
Целуешь ее, шепчешь на ушко: «любимая»,
А она тебе в ответ – «партнерка».
Ну после такого у любой упадет.
И больше не встанет.
Ты в курсе, что они подмышки не бреют?

Девочки, бросайте курить –
Целовать вас неприятно.
Если у вас есть проблемные места на теле –
Драпируйте их одеждой.
Набухались – ведите себя прилично
И берегите свою пилотку от членоходов.

Женщина – это искусство
Излучать любовь, тепло и сексуальность
В жестоком и холодном
Мире машин и мужчин.

And at my side I would prefer to have
A well-put-together, real woman.

And that's why I absolutely would never date a feminist:
You kiss her, whisper into her ear, "my love,"
And she responds: "your partner."
After something like that anyone could go limp.
And never get hard again.
Are you aware that they don't shave their armpits?

Girls, quit smoking—
Kissing you is unpleasant.
If you have problematic body parts—
Drape your clothing accordingly.
Got drunk? Behave yourself
And protect your socket from plugboys.

Woman is the art
Of radiating love, warmth and sexuality
In the cold, cruel
World of machines and men.

Kevin M. F. Platt on Translating Ekaterina Simonova

In a recent reading I was asked if there were special challenges for me as a man in translating poetry written by a woman. I answered then that translation is always about stretching the bounds of your own your subjectivity. I'd like to add here that gender is the least of the challenges we face these days as translators. What about space?

This year it has been: flip open the laptop, put on your headphones, fire up Zoom, and translate.

For the first time, I've translated a living poet whom I've never met in person, Ekaterina Simonova. I have never seen her poetry on a physical, printed page. I have heard her voice only as registered by a microphone, transmitted across continents and oceans as a stream of bits and bytes, and reconstituted by a tiny speaker in my ear.

I'm still not certain about how I feel about this. I miss gathering in the little frame house for the poetry translation symposium at my university, sitting in a circle for hours with poets and translators and trading words about trading words.

But there is a certain magic at work here. I haven't gone this long without visiting Russia for thirty years. Like everyone else, I've been locked in for an age. But Ekaterina's electronically reproduced words in my computer and voice in my head have transported/translated me to Ekaterinburg (did they name the city after her?) and Nizhny Tagil (I did actually visit there, once upon a time). Meetings with her and the workshop with the other poets and translators in this project reassembled our fractured space and opened closed borders, at least for an hour or two inside my laptop.

I learned new words, like *shaika* (a little tub in a public bath) and *chlenokhody* (a challenge for this translator). Technically speaking, the slang registers of language were the biggest stumbling block in this poetry, which is chocabloc with reported speech and found speech, rendered with greater or lesser degrees of irony and distance from Ekaterina's own voice and social and lyric identity. I don't think there is an English word that corresponds to *pabl* (a public informational page—I rendered it as "insta," to get the sense of social-media jargon). How to build a natural, talky cadence around identity semaphores like these—that was the central challenge.

With Ekaterina, my subjectivity was stretched in completely new ways—geographically, politically, linguistically, and every which way. Full disclosure: I made sure to ask Polina Barskova to vet me (a cis-gender man) as a translator with Ekaterina before signing on to this project. I'm grateful she agreed to let me translate her beautiful, important poetry.

And I am looking forward to the time when she will come to my university and give a reading in the big hall in the little wood frame house.

Poems by Nikita Sungatov

TRANSLATED BY VALERIYA YERMISHOVA

NIKITA SUNGATOV is a poet and a coeditor of *Translit*, an influential literary journal based in Saint Petersburg. A graduate of the Maxim Gorky Literature Institute, Sungatov was short-listed for the 2015 Arkady Dragomoshchenko Award, where he is now a member of the curatorial team. His book, *Debutnaya kniga molodogo poeta* (*The Debut Book of the Young Poet*), was published in 2015, and his poetry and criticism have been published in *Vozdukh*, *syg.ma*, and elsewhere.

VALERIYA YERMISHOVA is a freelance French- and Russian-to-English translator based in the New York City area. She served as president of the New York Circle of Translators in 2015–2016 and currently teaches in the Hunter College Master of Arts in Translation and Interpreting program. She is the translator of Viktor Shklovsky's *Life of a Bishop's Assistant* and Sergey Kuznetsov's *The Round Dance of Water*.

[A MODERN POEM]

Когда началась пандемия,
он сразу понял:
это то, к чему он готовился всю свою жизнь.

В запылившемся сейфе
он нашел старые расчеты
и, разложив карты на столе: карты мира, ноутбук с треснувшим
      экраном,
эти таблицы, заполненные около тридцати
лет назад, табак, несколько пар очков, набор
медицинских масок... он сопоставил: официальные данные ВОЗ,
топ популярных запросов в google, свидетельства в социальных
      сетях,
собственные расчеты и то, что было в таблицах, о чем
написать здесь нельзя. Он понял,
что не ошибся.

Сев за руль старого Chevrolet,
в перчатках и маске, он поехал
к генералу Кузнецову, в город где был молодым
и где ряд искажений на фасадах больниц и
в пустующем доме на улице лейтенанта Петренко
все еще, как и всегда, заставляет работать память. Природа
стучала в тонированные стекла так непоэтично, так просто,
как радиоволны, которые скоро его предадут,
пока он будет спать. Этим все и закончится. В баре

в это время обычно никого, дублированный официант
вежливо интересуется, что принести. Котенок-мышонок
появляется здесь на секунду, только чтобы напомнить,
что мы все еще нужны друг другу. Больши объемы
информации свертываются в минимальные единицы,
для будущих поколений. *Нужно ли стать врагом, чтобы*

[A MODERN POEM]

When the pandemic began,
he knew right away:
he had been preparing for it his whole life.

He found the old calculations
in the dusty safe,
laid out the world map, a laptop with a cracked screen,
the tables filled out thirty or so
years ago, tobacco, a few pairs of eyeglasses and a pack
of medical masks on the table . . . compared the official data of the
    WHO,
the top Google searches, and testimonials on social media
with his own calculations and the contents of the tables, what
he couldn't write about here. He realized
that he wasn't mistaken.

He got behind the wheel of an old Chevrolet
in his gloves and mask and drove off
to see General Kuznetsov in the city where he was young,
with its host of distortions on hospital façades, in
the vacant house on Lieutenant Petrenko Street,
which, to this day, triggers the memory. Nature
knocked on the tinted glass so unpoetically, so simply,
like the radio waves that will shortly betray him
as he sleeps. That'll put an end to it all. The bar

is typically empty at that hour, the dubbed waiter
asks politely what he can bring him. Kitty-mousie
appears for a split second just to remind us
that all of us still need each other. Great volumes
of information are rolled up into minimal units
for future generations. *Must one become the enemy to*

победить его? – думает it, барабаня пальцами по столу
и, допивая ипу, *не устояв* перед этим соблазном, пишет:

a modern poem

I.

ʂʌɾpan kuɛ: maaha ɜːli ʃʊ: ʃʊ: ʃʊ:
peəp pƏp «pʌp-pʌp-piːip-pʌb-bed»
cɯʃ cɯʃ aːd gʌɣtɛʃiŋ ɸ'm'иəpɛ
ɠaʕu/uiːra ip ohainowʌstɔ ʃʊ:

ɮʌʃi ʉgaʃъŋъj p̪ra: ^__^ ʂʌɾpan
'alə 'alə 'alə kuku kuku
aiñüirua u: mok̥ vas beb beb ebəb
ti-si-oʊ-keɪ aɪ-si-oʊ-keɪ ti-si-oʊ-keɪ

pi ɛs ʃa ʃa

II.

ʂʌɾpan kuɛ: maaha ɜːli ʃʊ: ʃʊ: ʃʊ:
peəp pƏp «pʌp-pʌp-piːip-pʌb-bed»
cɯʃ cɯʃ ard gʌɣtɛʃiŋ ɸ'm'иəpɛ
ɠaʕu/uiːra ip ohainowʌstɔ ʃʊ:

ɮʌʃi ʉgaʃъŋъj p̪ra: ^__^ ʂʌɾpan
'alə 'alə 'alə kuku kuku
aiñüirua u: mok̥ vas beb beb ebəb
ti-si-oʊ-keɪ aɪ-si-oʊ-keɪ ti-si-oʊ-keɪ

pi ɛs ʃa ʃa

Как бы ни был этот стишок прозрачен, пора было уходить:
какие-то мутные персонажи за соседним столиком
подозрительно что-то отхлебывали из пиал
и переговаривались в духе:

overcome him? it thinks, drumming its fingers on the table, and, as it finishes its IPA, *can't resist* writing:

a modern poem

I.
ʂʌɾpan kuɞ: maaha ɜ:li ʃʊ: ʃʊ: ʃʊ:
peəp pƏp «pʌp-pʌp-pi:ip-pʌb-bed»
cɯf cɯf a:d gʌɣtɛfɨɳ ɸ'm'uэpэ
ʙ̥aʕu/ui:ra ip ohainowʌstɔ ʃʊ:

ɮʌɭɨ ʉgaʃъŋъj p̺ɽa: ^__^ ʂʌɾpan
ˈalə ˈalə ˈalə kuku kuku
aiñüirua u: mo̡k vas beb beb ebɜb
ti-si-oʊ-keɪ aɪ-si-oʊ-keɪ ti-si-oʊ-keɪ

pi ɛs ʃa ʃa

II.
ʂʌɾpan kuɞ: maaha ɜ:li ʃʊ: ʃʊ: ʃʊ:
peəp pƏp «pʌp-pʌp-pi:ip-pʌb-bed»
cɯf cɯf ard gʌɣtɛfɨɳ ɸ'm'uэpэ
ʙ̥aʕu/ui:ra ip ohainowʌstɔ ʃʊ:

ɮʌɭɨ ʉgaʃъŋъj p̺ɽa: ^__^ ʂʌɾpan
ˈalə ˈalə ˈalə kuku kuku
aiñüirua u: mo̡k vas beb beb ebɜb
ti-si-oʊ-keɪ aɪ-si-oʊ-keɪ ti-si-oʊ-keɪ

pi ɛs ʃa ʃa

Despite how transparent this poem was, it was time to bail:
at the next table over, some shady characters
glugged something suspiciously from ceramic bowls,
exchanging words along the lines of:

- Борислав Юрьевич, я до тебя пытаюсь донести простую мысль:
прибыль либо есть, либо ее нет. Я в последнее время сильно
изменился,
и это не связано с твоим появлением в нашей фирме, я тебя
по-своему уважаю,
но, скорее, с возрастом жизнь становится несколько проще и
понятнее . . .

(и т. д.)

It идет по локации, напоминающей *Nochnoy Berlin*,
хотя это, конечно, не он. Шпионы за каждым углом, беспокоиться
легитимно. Бомбы-овечки падают. Обычно в подобных
ситуациях я закидываюсь
успокоительными, но в данном конкретном случае это было
трудновыполнимо.

Сверить данные и поехать дальше, генерал Кузнецов
гладит довольного серого кота на диване, поглядывая
на часы в форме гигантского золотого яйца. Их изготовил
какой-то маэстро из Франции, которого вскоре убили глухонемые,
вставили в горло секатор.

Фонари мрачно перемигиваются, это что-то напоминает тебе,
но что именно? Многие вещи, увы, остаются загадкой
даже после того сверхкраткого мига, когда *вдруг* понимаешь *все*.

Что беспокоит тебя, кроме выстрелов вдалеке?

Взять какао, скорее вернуться в машину, уснуть и поехать.
Сигарета-зима сделает мягким путь.

Dois-je devenir l'ennemi pour le vaincre,
il pense (этот фрагмент не успели перевести:
видишь ли, делали в пятницу, бары спешили закрыться).

Borislav Yuryevich, I'm trying to get this basic idea across to you:
either there's profit or not. I've changed a lot lately,
and it's got nothing to do with your joining our company, I still
respect you in my own way,
it's just that, as I get older, life becomes simpler and more
comprehensible somehow . . .

(and so forth)

It is walking along a site that recalls Nighttime Berlin,
although it's not him, of course. Spies lurk behind every corner, it
is legitimately
worried. Bomb-ewes fall everywhere. Usually at such times,
I take sedatives, but it wasn't feasible at this juncture.

Compare the data and keep driving, General Kuznetsov
is stroking a satisfied cat on the couch, glancing
at the watch shaped like a giant golden egg. It was made
by some maestro in France, who was soon killed by the deaf and dumb;
They stuck shearers in his throat.

Streetlamps blink gloomily at each other, it reminds you of something,
but what exactly? Alas, many things remain a mystery
even after very brief moment when, *suddenly*, you understand
everything.

What are you worried about, besides the shots ringing in the
distance?

Grab a hot chocolate, quickly return to the car, take a nap, and start
driving.
The cigarette-winter will sweeten the road.

Dois-je devenir l'ennemi pour le vaincre,
il pense (they didn't have time to translate this snippet:
see, they did it on a Friday, the bars were about to close . . .).

Вскоре it едет дальше, и мы с облегчением выдыхаем.

Когда it тяжело засыпает, то вспоминает
одно стихотворение из «Антологии русской поэзии XXI века»,
составленной по заказу
Министерства культуры, но it не знает, точно ли помнит его.

Вот оно:

Как тебя водили туда-сюда
по темным подвалам, жестоко пытали, но никогда
ты меня не покинешь, потому что сдохнешь, и это
помни о смерти всегда.

Как тебя снимали на видео для меня
("забери меня", "выкупи меня", и так далее), но
никто не даст ни рубля
за твое возвращение, детка, голубка, соска моя, божественное
     вино.

Как про это писала Линор Горалик
(говорят, она в Тель-Авиве большой начальник,
где все время взрывы гремят).

И когда ты вернешься в свой райский сад,
и когда твои звери меня пленят
и наставят палки на мозжечок
(ведь во рву остался один волчок),
прежде чем уничтожить, пойми наконец меня.

Как когда мы втроем убивали тебя,
это было смешно, так приказала партия,
и потом нажрались и упали вниз,
а наутро пели, дешевка, блюз,

Soon, it gets on its way and we heave a sigh of relief.

As it falls asleep with difficulty, it remembers
a poem from the *Anthology of 21st-Century Russian Poetry*
commissioned by
the Ministry of Culture, but can't say how accurate his memory is.

Here it is:

How they led you back and forth
through dark basements, torturing you cruelly, but you'll never
leave me because you'd croak, so
never forget about the death thing.

How they videotaped you for me
("get me out of here," "pay for me," and so on), but
no one would give a ruble
for your ransom, my child, my dove, my chickenhead, my ambrosial
    wine.

How Linor Goralik wrote about this,
they say she's a big boss in Tel Aviv,
explosions going off nearby somewhere.

And when you're back in your garden paradise
and your beasts take me captive
and place sticks in my brain,
after all, there is no one left in the ditch besides wolfy,
before you destroy me, you must understand me at last.

Like that time that the three of us were killing you,
it was funny, we had an order from the Party,
then, we got wasted and hit rock bottom
and in the morning, we sang the blues—so cheesy,

постоянно что-то происходило,
а над небом звездочка восходила.

Что можно сказать об этом тексте? Что нужно сказать? Субъект
насилия в нем помещен в сеттинг популярного стихотворения
Линор Горалик, которое, в свою очередь, написано на полях
евангельского сюжета. Другой очевидный претекст —
стихотворение Анны Горенко «Тело за мною ходило тело...»
Стихотворение связывает множество тем: государство и
маскулинный субъект; христианство и иудаизм; современная
поэзия и литературный быт; Арабо-израильская война и
Большой террор; насилие и медиа; насилие и идеология;
насилие и священное; насилие и его романтизация; и еще; и
еще. Какое отношение все это имеет друг к другу? Кто говорит
в этом стихотворении? А кто говорит прямо сейчас? Чтобы
избежать неудобного вопроса, нужно заставить повторить его
несколько раз, а потом объявить банальностью и штампом.

– как найти вас? в каких вы координатах? –
                          спрашивает ресничка
                            красивую звездочку.
                                  – здесь так неуютно...
речные животные
        слушают
                школу потоков,
                        все медленно возвращается,
включая вечерние прикосновения
                психоактивистов
                        под новогодней елкой...
It
        плывет
                по России,
                        как в каком-то комедийном
                                блокбастере 2010-х,
                                        разные гэги
                                                туманят ему башку,

there was always something happening
and a little star went up in the sky.

What can be said about this text? What needs to be said? A
violent criminal is placed in the setting of a popular poem by
Linor Goralik, which, in turn, was written on the margins of an
evangelical plot. Another obvious precursor is Anna Gorenko's
My Body Followed Me My Body . . . The poem is bound together
by a number of concepts: the State and the masculine subject;
Christianity and Judaism; contemporary poetry and literary reality;
the Arab-Israeli conflict and the Great Terror; violence and the
media; violence and ideology; violence and the sacred; violence
and the romanticization of it; and so on and so forth. What is the
connection between these concepts? Who is the narrator in this
poem? And who is speaking right now? To avoid having to answer
an uncomfortable question, you must ask your interlocutor to
repeat it a few times, then declare it a banality and a cliché.

how can I find you? what are your coordinates?
                the eyelash asks
                    a beautiful star,
                        I feel so uncomfortable here . . .
and the river faunae listen
              to the school of flows,
                  everything's slowly returning,
including the evening touches
            of psychoactivists
                  under the New Year's tree . . .
It is sailing
        down Russia as in some comedy
                blockbuster of the 2010s
                gags of all sorts
                    fog up its brain.

кадры сменяют друг друга: вот
                 it
          с бокалом шампанского на корабле Брюсов;

вот
     it
          в рабочем доме зимой в Ленобласти;
                                    it
               навещает родителей в Магнитогорске;
голоса
          чаек
               разрезают звуки прибоя в 6.00 am;
                         it
                    впервые
                              берет на руки малыша;

it
     в костюме снежинки
                    на kinky party;
it
     прячется от отца;
                    она
               клянется себе: это
                                   не повторится;

it
  кричит
          «Россия без Путина»
               на Центральной площади;
                    ветер
                         лущует волосы
                              телефонному террористу;
все обойдется;
          не мысли штампами;
                    все так живут;
                         не следует упрощать;

Frames flicker one after another: here's
       it
           with a glass of champagne on the ship *Bryusov*;

Here's
    it
       in a poorhouse in the winter in Leningrad Oblast;
               it
            is visiting its parents in Magnitogorsk;
seagulls'
      voices
          cut through the sounds of crashing waves at 6am;
             it
              picking up a baby
                    for the first time;

it
    in the costume of a snowflake
              at a kinky party;
it
    hiding from father;
        she
          swears to herself this
               won't ever happen again;

it
 screaming
   "Russia without Putin"
       in the main square;
          the wind
             thrashing the hair of
                the telephone terrorist;
everything will be fine;
     don't reason in clichés;
         everyone lives this way;
            don't make things easier;

it
участвует в акции
«Коллективных действий»;
бурит скважину
в спецовке и каске;
мы садимся в автомобиль
и едем
на каникулы в город,
где ряд искажений на фасадах больниц
и в пустующем доме
на улице лейтенанта Петренко
все еще, как и всегда,
заставляет работать память;

горят огоньки;
популярная музыка еле слышно играет по радио,
мы смеемся, как смеются обычно дети, узнавая знакомое
в незнакомом. Играем в карты. Раскрываем секреты друг
другу. Примеряем маски. Дорога будет размыта, когда
мы о ней вспомним. Как и все остальное. Шарпан. Сон
починит ускользающий свет. Говорят, на юге такое до сих
пор возможно. Не думай, просто дыши. Мысль находится
в другой мысли, а та — в третьей, как можно мыслить, не
захлебываясь? Рассказываем, что помним. Это немного,
а будет еще меньше. Ностальгия подкатывает к горлу на
соседней улице, та не издергалась вопреки ожиданиям властей.
Молимся одновременно, но никто не признается в этом,
даже когда мы шутим. Тоннель и огонь. Огонь и тоннель.
Когда началась пандемия. Сложно придумать хуже начало для
текста, написанного в 2020. По сути, я тоже была неправа. Не
надо рассказывать о случившемся, это может погубить его
репутацию и карьеру. Он хороший.Воспоминание о жажде
приходит вкруговую. Как утолить ее, если идут часы? Память
надрезана. Еще несколько мгновений, и она порвется. Брызги
ударят в лицо. Спазм охватит гортань. Гемоглобин окислится
до соляно-кислого гематина. Воды омоют легкие наши души.

it

　　　is taking part

　　　　　　　　in the Collective Actions Group;

　　　　　　　　　　　drilling a borehole

　　　　　　　　　　　　　　　in a hardhat and coveralls;

we get in the car

　　　　　and drive off

　　　　　　　　　　to vacation in the city

　　　　　　　　　　　　　　with a host of distortions on hospital façades,

in the vacant house

　　　　　　on Lieutenant Petrenko Street,

　　　　　　　　　　　　　which, to this day,

　　　　　　　　　　　　　　　　　triggers the memory;

the lights gleam;

　　　　　pop music plays barely audibly on the radio, we laugh as
children do when they find something familiar in the unfamiliar.
We play cards. We reveal secrets to each other. Try on masks. By
the time we recall the road, it'll be washed out. Like everything
else. A *sharpan*. Sleep will rectify the fading light. They say this is
still possible in the South. Don't think, just breathe. One thought
is found in another and the second in the third, how's it possible
to think without getting overwhelmed? We recount what we
remember. It's not much and there'll be still less. On the next street
over, nostalgia rises up to the throat, which is not overstrained,
despite the authorities' expectations. We pray at the same time, but
neither one of us admits to it, even when we're kidding. A tunnel
and a fire. A fire and a tunnel. *When the pandemic began.* It's hard to
think of a worse way to begin a poem written in 2020. To be honest,
I was also in the wrong. I shouldn't talk about what happened, it
could ruin his reputation and career. He's a good guy. The memory
of the thirst comes full circle. How can I quench it if the clock is
ticking? My memory has been slit. A few more moments and it'll
burst right open. Splashes will hit me in the face. My voice box
will be gripped by spasms. My hemoglobin will be oxidized into
hydrochloric hematin. Waters will wash over our light souls.

«Разве любовь — не чудо?» –
    спешно вбивает it в телефон,
        когда наша тачка стремительно бросается в Волгу.

Как соотносятся аффект и институт? В какой-то момент этот вопрос стал самым главным. Аффекты пронзают мое тело, и, чтобы оно стояло ровно, необходим институт. Институт придает форму аффекту, но вместе с тем он и искажает его, отсеивая тот избыток, который приносит наслаждение. Но наслаждение разрушительно, и поэтому нужен институт — как то, что установит границы моему наслаждению и не даст мне уничтожить себя и всех вас заодно. Ограничивая аффект, институт сохраняет намек на тот избыток, который он в себе несет. Это поэзия. Строгая форма, точнее, не обязательно строгая, любая служит искусственным ограничителем аффекту и в то же время индексом, указывающим на то, что обрезано. Вот чем отличается поэзия от прозы: в основе поэзии есть формальное ограничение, структурный принцип, который может быть и не сразу заметен, отсекающий сказанное от говоримого, оставляющий желанию место за границей текста; прозаический текст обманывает себя, якобы он полон и полностью самотождественен, это всегда ложь. Присяга верности определенной строгой форме вызывала во мне смесь иронии и почтения: подобное ограничение совершенно глупо, зачем себя ограничивать, и в то же время это спасительная глупость. Субъект есть форма.

Я есть то, чем я не являюсь: это этика поэтического.

Вот что всегда волновало меня: случайность того, что я называю "собой" — своих мыслей, ценностей, чувств, влюбленностей и страхов, идей, телесных реакций. Уже позже появились буддизм и психоанализ, ницшеанство и марксизм, Хайдеггер и квир-теория — все это уже лишь подтверждало детскую интуицию, что то, как я явлен в мир, произвольно и не является мной в полной мере. Я втиснуто в искусственные ограничители и

"Isn't love such a miracle?"
      it hurriedly types into its phone
            as our car plunges into the Volga at full speed.

What's the relationship between "an affect" and "the Institution"?
At one point, this question became the most crucial. Affects
impale my body and I need the Institution to keep it upright. The
Institution gives shape to an affect but also distorts it, eliminating
the excess that brings pleasure. But pleasure's destructive, which
is why I need the Institution to set limits on my pleasure and not
let me destroy myself and all of you with me. As it curbs an affect,
the Institution preserves a soupçon of the inherent excess of the
former. That is poetry. A strict form, or rather, not necessarily
strict, but any form that serves as an artificial constraint for an
affect and, at the same time, an index that specifies what has
been cut. That is the difference between poetry and prose: at
the basis of poetry lies formal constraint, a structural principle
which may not even be immediately apparent and which separates
what has been said from what has been spoken, leaving room for
desires beyond the scope of the text; a prosaic text deludes itself
into thinking it is complete and completely selfidentical, which
is always a lie. A sworn loyalty to a certain strict form would
elicit in me a mix of irony and reverence: a limitation of this
kind is downright foolish, why limit yourself, but even so, it's a
redemptive foolishness. The subject is the form.

I am what I'm not: that is the ethic of the poetic.

That is what always preoccupied me: the arbitrariness of what I
call "myself"—of my own speech, feelings, thoughts, infatuations
and fears, ideas and physical reactions. Only later came Buddhism
and psychoanalysis, Nietzscheanism and Marxism, linguistics and
neurobiology—all that only confirmed my childhood hunch that
the way I appear in the world is arbitrary and isn't fully me. "I"
am squeezed into artificial constraints and am a mere index of my
being, the same way that poetry serves as a testimony of a desire

являюсь лишь индексальным знаком своего бытия, в той же мере, что и поэзия является свидетельством желания, специально забытого за границами текста и колотящегося снаружи, стремясь попасть внутрь, но никогда не проникающего.

Если солидарность между всеми нами возможна, то лишь основанная на этом знании, знании своей случайности.

Какой хорошей бывает юность!

Когда с утра пускаешь день на самотек
                          и не идешь на экзамен.

И желание *определенным образом* вписаться
                          в символическую структуру,
определенным образом прописаться
                          в публичной речи
еще нигде не жмет, как и пальто на пол-размера больше
                    (с кедровыми шишками в карманах).

А вот амбиция лихо бежит ранней осенью по набережной,
                    начитавшись чужих биографий,
          насмотревшись желаний в кино. Что организует ее?
То, что так приятно вспоминать.

То, что фиксирует
          невыносимость одиночества, изоляции в
                          комнате с книгами.
И то, что почему-то называется "любовь".
И Нева, и анархия, и пока что отсутствие толерантности
                    и абстинентного синдрома.

that has been intentionally forgotten beyond the scope of the text
and is outside banging on the door, desperate to get in, but never
gains entry.

If solidarity between us all is possible, then only on the basis of this
knowledge, the knowledge of our arbitrariness.

How wonderful youth can be!

When you let the day go where it wants
                                        and skip the exam.

And no part of you is yet stifled

by the desire to inscribe yourself *in a certain way*
                                        in the symbolic structure,
to record yourself *in a certain way*
                                in public discourse
just as you aren't stifled by your overcoat a half size too big,
                                (with pine cones in your pockets).

Now watch ambition run boldly down the quay in early fall,
                                having read others' biographies,
                        having watched too many movies about desires.
                                        What gets it going?
Things that are nice to recall.

Things that capture
                the excruciating loneliness and isolation in your room
                                        with your books.
And that which, for some reason, is known as "love."
And the Neva River, and anarchy, and, for the time being, the lack
                                                of tolerance
                                and the abstinence syndrome.

Такая тема! –
        говорит *it* случайный попутчик. –
        Эта тема уже отработана. Будет много других.

Поезд едет по черной Транссибирской магистрали,
        в нем мы трясемся, осколки чужих рассказов,
           смотрим на время, которое остановилось,
               как лирично все это.

– неужели ты правда считаешь, что все постоянно врут и
иного бытия нет? –
        говорит лучик веточке

– почему же? еще есть ритм, –
           говорит лепесток травинке

– мне кажется, it *хочет открыть отношения, –*
              шепчет травинка
              лучику солнца,

обнимающему твой порез от бритвы
        в миг,
           когда ты думаешь (старомодно),
             что настоящий анализ поэзии
              доступен только лингвисту.

Awesome topic!
       a chance traveler tells *it.*
             This topic has been exhausted. There'll be many others.

The train is traveling down the black Trans-Siberian Railway,
      inside it, fragments of others' tales pour boiling water into
                          plastic packaging
       and look at the time, which has stopped,
            how lyrical all this is.

do you really think that everyone's always lying and there is no other
    way of being?
           says the ray of sun to the little branch

why so? there is also rhythm,
          says the leaf to the blade of grass

I think it *wants to start a relationship,*
                whispers the blade of grass
              to the ray of sun

that wraps itself around your razor cut
        the moment
           you think (the old-fashioned way)
            that a true analysis of poetry
              accessible only to a linguist.

Детское Стихотворение

расстояний не существует, пишет львовский в своих стихах,
это трудно, признаться, слышать, без переченья на устах,
ведь у нас есть мудрая книжка, и мы в ней прочитали так,
что в стихах, если книжке верить, расстояния не пустяк,

что немного будет лукавством просто брать и сближать имена:
между ними не только пространство, но и разные времена,
между, скажем, «кошкой» и «ложкой» расстояние в сотни лет,
и придется приврать немножко, чтоб сказать «расстояний
    нет»

синхронии не существует, ошибался старик соссюр,
никогда не встретит поребрик свой французский собрат
    бордюр,
и не встретятся, невозможно, жак руссо и наполеон,
мы живем в языке, то есть в ложном искривлении всех времен

мы событие называем тем, что было у наших мам,
а потом в словах исчезаем. нет доверия этим словам!
что случилось, когда в романе льва толстого явился он?
князь андрей был смертельно ранен, и язык превратился в сон

знаю точно, что мне приснится, этой ночью увижу я,
как ты всех побеждаешь, львица, а с тобою твои друзья
и с тобою твои подруги, и собаки, и стая птиц,
и в поэзии нет расстояний, и в фантазии нет границ

будь, король язык, обезглавлен! ты, кричим мы, голый король!
в нашем кукольном уличном театре у тебя пораженца роль!
мимо знака фонемы граммы мы пойдем на прямой протест
и скрепившимися телами субверсивный исполним жест

CHILDREN'S POEM

There is no such thing as distances, Lvovsky writes in his poems,
I admit, I find this hard to hear without offering some back talk,
After all, we have all read a grown-up book that says
Distances are nothing to sneer at, if we take it literally,

It would be a bit facetious to simply take names, place them side by
    side:
There is not only space between them, they belong to different
    periods of time,
For example, there's a span of centuries between a "cat" and a "hat"
And you would be lying a little if you said: "distances, ain't no such
    thing."

There is no such thing as synchronicity, old man Saussure got it all
    wrong,
A suburban curb won't ever meet its big-city counterpart, the *bord
    du trottoir*,
And there won't ever be a meeting between Napoleon and Jacques
    Rousseau,
We are living in language—that is, in a funhouse mirror of all time

We call an event by a name that describes what our mothers had
    happen to them,
Then, we disappear in these words, we cannot give credence to them!
What happened when he turned up in a novel by Leo Tolstoy?
Prince Andrei was fatally wounded and the tongue turned into a
    dream

I know for certain what I'll dream of tonight,
I'll see you defeating everyone, Lioness, your friends by your side,
Your girlfriends, your dogs, and a flock of birds with you,
And there are no distances in poetry, the imagination knows no bounds

и не будет ретроактивной
травмы боли вины
и очистятся от первосцены
наши взрослые сны

знаю точно, что мне приснится, этой ночью увижу я,
как ты всех побеждаешь, львица, а с тобою твои друзья
и с тобою твои подруги, и собаки, и стая птиц,
и в поэзии нет расстояний, и в фантазии нет границ

May King Tongue be beheaded! We cry, "You're an emperor with
    no clothes!"
In our traveling marionette theater, you've been given the loser's role!
Past the punctuation mark the phoneme the *gramma*, off we go to
    protest directly
And we'll bind our bodies together to perform a subversive gesture

And there won't be retroactive
Trauma pain guilt
Our adult dreams will be cleansed
Of the primal scene

I know for certain what I'll dream of tonight,
I'll see you defeating everyone, Lioness, your friends by your side,
Your girlfriends, your dogs, and a flock of birds with you,
And there are no distances in poetry, the imagination knows no bounds

ПОДРАЖАНИЕ ВЛ. ХОДАСЕВИЧУ

Тем утром я проснулся слишком поздно.
Ни солнце, ни мобильный телефон
Меня не разбудили. Melancholia,
Старинная высокая болезнь,
Меня в объятиях Морфея заточила.
Мне снилось, будто нету Бытия.

Глупейший сон! Какое это счастье,
Что Парменид писал поэмы. Бытие
Не может «быть» или «не быть», оно не вещь,
Оно – концепт, тюрьма для смысла, а реальность –
Всегда изменчива, и то, что было «кошкой»
В той итерации, уже не будет «кошкой»
Одно движенье лапками спустя.

И оттого невыносима речь,
Пока она не обретает право
Перформативно устанавливать закон.

Я думал о тебе, и я проснулся.
Цветы стояли в вазе на столе.
Мне голос был: в ином варианте жизни
Ложись в двенадцать, просыпайся в восемь,
Как все поэты, изучай античность.
И изучай генеративную грамматику.
Никакого прагматического языкознания!

. . . Каким же текстом можно показать,
Как измерения мерцают друг сквозь друга?..

*

After Vladislav Khodasevich

That morning, I woke up too late.
Neither the sun nor my cell phone
Had roused me. Melancholia,
That antediluvian, noble affliction,
Confined me to Morpheus's arms.
I dreamt that there was no such thing as Being.

What a preposterous dream! It's our great luck
Parmenides wrote poems. Existence
Can't "be" or "not be," it's not a thing,
It is a concept, a prison for meaning, while reality
Is always changeable, and what was once a "cat"
In that version of it will no longer be a "cat."
Only a stirring of the paws going forward.

That is what makes speech unbearable
Until it acquires the right
To performatively establish law.

I thought of you and I woke up.
The flowers were standing in a vase on the table.
A voice spoke to me: In another reality,
Go to bed at midnight, get up at eight,
Study antiquity like all the poets,
And study generative grammar.
No practical language skills!

... What sort of text can I use to show
The way dimensions gleam through each other? ...

*

[далее – фрагмент, написанный в другом стиле. без него было
    бы *лучше*]

*

говорят
«да, он сексист, зато превосходный аналитик»

говорят
«любые средства хороши в борьбе с полицейским государством»

говорят
«мы поддерживаем ЛГБТ»

говорят
«помните стихотворение Пазолини?»

они
называют себя «гетеросексуалы»

они
просто боятся любить

*

ты похож на Сашу Скидана,
говорит она

про любовь, похожую на сон,
говорит Полина Аронсон

падающее толкай до дна,
поет Луна

положи мне палец в рот
(и наоборот)

[farther down is a fragment written in a different style. the poem
would be *better* without it]

*

they say
"yes, he's a sexist, but he's an excellent pundit"

they say
"the ends justify the means when combating a police state"

they say
"we support the LGBT movement"

they say
"remember Pasolini's poem?"

they
call themselves "heterosexuals"

they
are simply afraid to love

*

you look like Sasha Skidan,
she says

about an "Endless Love,"
utters Polina Aronson

push what is falling toward the bottom
croons the moon

put your finger in my mouth
(and vice versa)

*

Эрот не спит. Эрот читает йенских
Романтиков, поскольку точно знает:
В некаузальных просодических повторах
Живет Психея (Кстати, как она
Топологически размещена?)

На семантемах проступают раны,
И в языке потенциально есть,

(и потому мы об этом знаем)

Что Люба Соболь нашего тирана
Убьет – и сердце его съест.

Мы спим. Но и во сне, как говорит Монтлевич,
Мы реагируем на внешний свет
И движемся телами и вещами
Сквозь проясняющий освобождающий поток.

Спи, котик. Пусть война уйдет.

*

Eros isn't asleep. Eros is reading the Jena
Romantics because he knows for certain that
In the acausal prosodic repetitions
Dwells Psyche (by the way, how's she
Proportioned topologically?)

Wounds develop on semantemes
And it is likely that the tongue knows

(. . . and, hence, we know about it . . .)

That Lyuba Sobol will slay
Our tyrant—and eat his heart.

We are asleep. But in our sleep, too, as Montlevich says,
We react to ambient light
And move our bodies and our things
Through an illuminating, liberating flow.

Sleep, kitty. Let the war be over.

Valeriya Yermishova on Translating Nikita Sungatov

Not only do Nikita Sungatov's poems contain a myriad references to Russian political and cultural figures and the Soviet and Russian canon of songs and films, they also make nods to and directly quote other contemporary Russian poets. Some of these references are explained directly and others are less obvious. In the latter cases, the translator has to decide whether to leave the foreign references in the text—which I did in most cases—or adapt them to something more familiar to English speakers. I thought that the audience for these poems would either be familiar with these references or would be interested in learning more about them.

A section of "A Modern Poem" is styled after "Как в норе лежали они с волчком . . ." ["How they lay in the burrow together . . ."], a well-known poem by Linor Goralik, and mentions her by name. As in "Children's Poem," another poem featured here, there is a juxtaposition between childlike and sophisticated language, cartoonish images and adult themes. This section is written from the point of view of a kidnapper and includes the animal nickname "wolfy." Another small animal, kitty-mousie, makes a cameo in "A Modern Poem."

"Children's Poem" also contains a mix of childlike language and sophisticated themes. Given that the rhyme scheme and language are closer to those of Dr. Seuss, my colleagues suggested translations such as "a cat and a hat" and "spoon and moon." In this poem, the author repeatedly uses the imagery of the lion by referring to poet Stanislav Lvovsky, novelist Leo Tolstoy, and the Lioness, a woman who comes to the poet in his dreams in the guise of an action film heroine. Here, the poet is referring to a genre of films and cartoons about groups of female characters that battle villains.

Another recurring theme is the use of the French language, which is bolstered by references to Napoleon and Jean-Jacques Rousseau and to francophone Swiss linguist Ferdinand de Saussure. The Russian word for "curbside" is derived from the French word *trottoir* but applies only in cities and is contrasted here with the Russian word for small-town curbs, *поребрик*. Since we don't have this distinction in English, I tried to create it by using the French word as follows: "A suburban curb won't ever meet its big-city counterpart, the *bord du trottoir*."

"Children's Poem" refers to the concept of synchronicity, which was first introduced by analytical psychologist Carl Jung. It discusses the spiritual aspect of long-distance relationships, which allow for more dreaming in the absence of the beloved. The poet experiences closeness with his beloved when she visits him in dreams. The poem ends with the verse "And there are no distances in poetry, the imagination knows no bounds," celebrating the power of art and that of the imagination in bringing people closer together.

The third poem, "After Vladislav Khodasevich," picks up on the theme of the poet missing his beloved: he says that he thought of her just before awakening. The poem is named and styled after Vladislav Khodasevich (1886–1939), a Russian émigré poet with a joyful, light-as-gossamer style. Other public figures referenced in this poem are poet Aleksandr Skidan; political activist Lyuba Sobol (full name: Lyubov Sobol), whom the BBC wrote about in its coverage of Russian political protests in 2019; and Buddhist and art historian Vladimir Montlevich.

One of the challenges of translating this poem was maintaining consonance in a series of verses, one of which was the name of a well-known Russian ballad by singer Alla Pugacheva. I adapted it to "Endless Love," an American ballad by Diana Ross and Lionel Richie, because the Russian song has a lyric that says "I hope this love does not end." I lost the rhyme but compensated for it a few lines later with "croons the moon."

Nikita Sungatov's poems are firmly situated in the present and touch upon current issues, including the global pandemic and ongoing political events in Russia. A poem that didn't make it into this collection owing to its length, "Simple Poems," recounts a series of scenes that take place on the bridges and boulevards of Saint Petersburg, where the poet is currently based.

Afterword

Polina Sadovskaya

Building linkages between writers from the United States and Russia (and before that the Soviet Union) is a PEN America tradition with a long history. In 1991—the year of the Soviet Union's collapse—PEN America, together with CUNY's Hunter College and other partners (including Stolichnaya Vodka!), organized a conference entitled "Interpreting Each Other: Russian and American Literature in Translation." It was an important year to hold such a conference; Russian and American citizens and literary professionals had had little or no opportunity to meet in person and exchange ideas before the dissolution of the Soviet Union brought the hope of breaking that silence and sharing freely.

Thirty years later, after the emergence of the internet and coming of age of a generation that has never lived without it, the isolation of the past may seem simply impossible in such a connected world. However, slowly but steadily over the last twenty years of Russian President Vladimir Putin's rule, the Iron Curtain has been replaced by the Glass Wall: you can see through but cannot really get to the other side. The extreme difficulty of getting US visas for Russians inevitably reminds us of the time when travel abroad was almost impossible. In Russia, the government's "foreign agent" label for those interacting with the West has become the new "enemy of the people."

This anthology is the product of PEN America's "US/Russia Writers in Dialogue" project. Over the course of the last five years, the project has brought prominent American authors to Russia and brought established and emerging writers from Russia to the

United States. The goal of this exchange has been to ensure that the dialogue between the two countries continues despite the tireless efforts of state propaganda and political actors—sometimes on both sides—to stigmatize such interactions.

The COVID-19 crisis has only heightened the urgency of PEN America's mission to unite writers in celebrating literature and defending the right to free expression. Authoritarian leaders have seized on the pandemic to further infringe freedoms and in the name of public health. And because of global travel restrictions, PEN America had to transform its in-person exchange between American and Russian writers into a virtual one. The online collaboration still proved fruitful: in late 2020, we paired six Russian poets who have not been previously published in the US with six American translators who worked on a set of their poems under the careful guidance of the distinguished poet and scholar Polina Barskova. We even hosted a virtual workshop to help the poets and translators come up with solutions for complicated linguistic challenges as a group and forge personal connections.

Thanks to our partner publisher, Deep Vellum, readers in the US and the rest of the English-speaking world will have a glimpse into the world of contemporary Russian poetry. It is a genre that has traditionally flourished in trying times, and now, with the help of this project, also supported by Columbia University's Harriman Institute, we can contemplate this blossoming for ourselves. No two of the chosen poets are alike: they represent different styles, different forms, and different experiences; they are of different ages and from different regions within Russia. Each, though, tells stories that are silenced by official channels—stories that therefore are particularly worthy of the world's attention, and yours.